Panama City to F

CU00857507

Travels through S

By Jason Smart

First English edition published in 2013 by Smart Travel Publishing

Cover design by Ace Graphics

ASIN: B00FV49WK4
ISBN-13: 978-1493515059
ISBN-10: 1493515055

Smart, Jason J
Panama City to Rio de Janeiro: Travels through South America

For my parents, Jim and Monica Smart

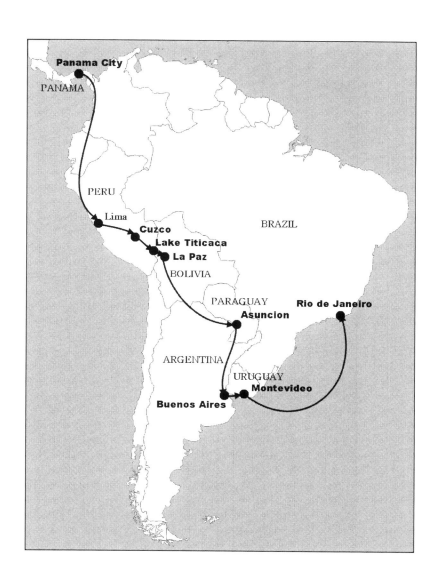

Contents

Chapter 1. Panama City: The start of the adventure

Interesting fact: The Panama hat originated in Ecuador.

We expected the skyscrapers but not the sheer numbers of them. Panama City was a jungle of glass and concrete: twisty ones, curvy ones, but mainly thin white ones. They were set against a backdrop of tropical jungle that overlooked the blue of the Pacific Ocean. It was as if we were in Miami or perhaps Hong Kong: certainly not Central America.

"I don't know anyone who has been to Panama," my wife said, smiling at the excitement of being on a brand new trip. "It sounds so...I don't know...exotic!"

We were sitting in the back of an airport taxi on our way to the hotel. It was late evening, the sun already making its way over the horizon, casting a dull orange glow over some of the architecture. Angela was staring outside, perhaps trying to decipher some of the words on the Spanish billboards. Before arriving in Latin America, both of us had tried to learn a little Spanish. I'd persevered for longer, soon establishing my favourite phrase in the entire language: *una cerveza para mi, por favor* – one beer for me, please. On the flight across the Atlantic, Angela had grown weary of me saying it over and over, especially with the added flourish of a Spanish accent cultivated from watching endless episodes of Speedy Gonzales as a child. *Una cerveza para mi, arriba, ARRIBA!*

It *was* exciting being in Panama. Even the eleven hours we'd spent cooped up inside a KLM jet had not put a dampener on our mood. The start of a new trip is always full of eager anticipation; looking forward to the things we would see, the new cultures we'd experience and collecting tales we would be able to tell people back home.

And the planning had been fun too. It always was. Where should we go? What should we see? And how should we travel between them? As part of our hectic itinerary, we'd already factored in some high-end tourist attractions: places like Machu Picchu, Lake Titicaca, Copacabana Beach and of course, watching a tango dance in Buenos Aires, but we were also going to visit some often overlooked places in South America, namely Paraguay and Uruguay. Yes, the thought of what was to come was an exciting proposition.

Then there was the flurry of activity involving travel vaccinations. Would we need rabies jabs? What about hepatitis B and yellow fever? And wasn't La Paz notorious for altitude sickness? All of these things required careful consideration. But in the end, we formulated a plan and then booked a series of flights. And now here we were, at the start of it all, in Panama City.

2

"I should never have listened to you," said Angela the next morning. "I knew this would happen. I just knew!"

I wiped the sweat from my forehead and shook my T-shirt. A smidgeon of wind to cool myself down would be a welcome distraction. The street was busy, full of shops opening up for the day. I looked at the map and then at the street names around. Nothing matched up. We were lost and it was all my fault.

Forty minutes earlier, after finishing breakfast, it had been my suggestion that we head outside for a quick wander around. I wanted to take a photo of a skyscraper I'd seen the previous evening. From the back seat of the taxi, the skyscraper had seemed close to our hotel, possibly just around the corner.

"But we've got a tour in an hour," Angela reminded me. "The guy is picking us up at 8.30."

"I know. It's plenty of time."

"What if we get lost?"

"We won't. I've got a map."

Despite my wife's reservations, we hit the busy streets of downtown Panama City. We were soon walking past a couple of casinos on the same street as our hotel. All would be opening for business later that day, flashing their neon well until the early hours. Around and among them, bars and restaurants were being cleaned in preparation for the day's festivities – tablecloths wiped, floors mopped, and buckets of water sloshed out over the pavements. Numerous street stalls were cooking up fried food and were doing a brisk business, serving commuters on their way to work.

Skyscrapers loomed overhead in all directions but I couldn't see the one I was looking for. But it had to be nearby, I reasoned. Maybe around the next corner. Or the one after that. I pretended I knew where I was going, my eyes greedily searching out a street name I could take my bearings from.

"Jesus, it's humid," I said, as we crossed a street full of angry traffic, all beeping, all furiously trying to push into lanes that were not there. Old buses full of Panamanians trundled along, thick plumes of black smoke escaping from their vertical exhausts. Most had been gaudily painted in bright reds, greens, yellows and blues. Others had pictures of animals emblazoned across them – jaguars, lizards and eagles seemed a popular choice, but so did chickens and fairytale creatures. One truck had *The Punisher* decorated on its side panel. Judging by the looks of the people cooped up inside, it was living up to its name.

We rounded another bend, arriving at a wide boulevard that looked like a busy New York avenue. Yellow cabs sped by, passing designer shops and plush hotels.

"There it is," I said triumphantly, finally catching sight of the corkscrew-shaped skyscraper. It was a few blocks away, poking over the top of some other buildings. I suggested to Angela that we try to get nearer. With over twenty-five minutes before we had to be back to the hotel, we had plenty of time.

We stood beneath the Revolution Tower (or the F & F Tower, as it is sometimes called), and marvelled. Well I did, though Angela seemed fairly taken with it too. It was without doubt one of the most impressive buildings I'd ever seen. It could easily have joined the skyline in cities such as Hong Kong or Dubai. The way the sun caught its many angles was nothing short of mesmerising. It looked like the end of a screw, but a giant screw made of blue glass. How engineers had constructed such a thing was beyond my comprehension.

I noticed Angela studying her watch, which meant that it was time to move on. I took a few more photos and then looked at the map. I soon noticed a shortcut that would get us back to the hotel and pointed it out to my wife. She looked but offered no comment, which I took as assent.

Ten minutes later, Angela and I were doing a merry little dance that involved glaring, swearing and temperatures flaring. With the map rendered useless, we were walking aimlessly again, sweat erupting from my forehead. We rounded a corner where I stopped a man for directions. Like most Panamanians, he was mestizo, half-Amerindian and half-white (a legacy left over from the Spanish invaders). He claimed to have not even heard of our hotel. I thanked him anyway and trudged onwards. Angela's mood darkened to storm status.

"I told you we should have gone back the way we came!" she scolded. Lightning flashed in her eyes. "We need to be back at the hotel in five minutes! We're going to be late because of you!"

"I know, I'm sorry. But what can I do? Throw myself in front of a bus?"

"That would be a start."

Wiping the sweat from my brow, we rushed along a busy road full of banks and more designer shops. I was looking in vain for any landmark I could get my bearings from. The only thing I recognised was the twisty tower, which had got us into the mess in the first place. In desperation, I stuck my arm into the road, in the hope that one of the yellow taxis would come to our assistance. None did, and so I stopped to glare at the pathetic map again. Why had I decided to put my trust in it, I fumed? Why indeed? Like many *Lonely Planet* maps, it was utterly useless, out of date and threadbare on meaningful points of reference. Wondering whether to scrunch it into a ball and throw it as far as I could, I glanced around and noticed something. It was tucked up a little side street just along from us.

"There's the hotel," I said, jubilantly. Angela spun her head and saw it. I was already smiling and breathing easily for the first time in a while. "See I told you we'd get back in time." A minute later, we entered its air-conditioned interior. Normal service had resumed.

4

"Hi, you must be Jason, and you must be Angela," said the man wearing a Panama Trails T-shirt. He shook our hands and introduced himself as John, our guide for the next four hours. He was a tall, thin man in his mid-thirties who possessed a friendly smile and an American accent.

"You don't sound like you're from Panama," I said.

"No I'm not," John answered as we made our way to the exit. "I was born in Michigan, raised in Florida, but moved to Panama City nine years ago to marry my Panamanian wife. I love it here. There are not many countries I can think of where you can have jungle one day, mountains the next, a tropical beach the day after that, and then, to end with, a modern city full of skyscrapers. Do you know it's the fourth most popular country for US retirees, and in 2012, it was voted the happiest city on Earth?"

We climbed into the brightly-coloured Panama Trails mini-van. It was splashed with cartoons of indigenous animals, including turtles, monkeys and tropical fish. Angela and I took our seats in the back and fastened out seatbelts.

"Okay then," said John, from the driver's seat. "First stop is the Panama Canal. We should get there just in time to see a few ships going through. It might be busy with other tour groups though. We'll see."

John pulled into the manic traffic of downtown Panama City. It still reminded me a little of New York because of the skyscrapers and buzzing yellow cabs, but unlike New York, the traffic was a free-for-all. Within minutes of setting off, a large 4x4 cut in front of us, causing John to brake heavily. He gave the other driver a blast of his horn. From the back, Angela and I smiled nervously.

John smirked. "You know what? When I first arrived in Panama, I was scared to death about driving. For two weeks I thought I was gonna get killed by these mad idiots on the road. It's not like in the States or in Europe, where drivers are courteous, and might let you out from a junction. No, in Panama, they don't give an inch. But now my wife says I drive as bad as the rest of them."

As we threaded our way towards the canal, we drove through some less sparkly parts of Panama City, mainly rundown apartment blocks and honking bus stations. People were standing at road junctions buying street food, or waiting to board the colourful buses. Yet even in the less salubrious parts of the city, the citizens looked happy. And why not? They were living in the richest country in Central America.

5

We eventually arrived at the canal, or rather a section of it called the Miraflores Locks, at just after 9am. Miraflores was one of three locks along the 80km waterway, and because of its proximity to Panama City, it had turned into a major tourist attraction.

To be honest, I wasn't really looking forward to seeing the canal. To me, it sounded dull. Why would I want to spend half an hour watching a ship going through a narrow stretch of water? But as Angela pointed out, we *had* to see it. Imagine the reaction of people back home if we failed to do so. *What?* they would say, *you went to Panama but didn't see the Panama Canal? Are you mad?* It was like flying to Sydney and not bothering to look at the Opera House.

"Like I said," John explained as we stepped outside, "at this time of day, there should be at least a couple of ships passing through. But what I'm more worried about is how busy the viewing platform will be. Come on, let's find out."

We followed him through the modern tourist entrance (thankfully with no queue) and then came to the viewing platform. John needn't have worried because it was almost empty. Only a young couple stood there, staring out at the waterway. "Good," John beamed. "We can bag the best spot."

He led us up some metal stairs and pointed to where we should stand. As we did so, we could hear a hubbub behind us somewhere. The noise grew louder as the doors opened to reveal a cauldron of tourists. Evidently, a large tour group had just arrived: a camera-toting horde that rampaged up the stairs to reach the best viewing position. Some of them had ice-creams.

"See what I mean?" John said, moving closer to us, allowing the newcomers into his space. "We timed it just right."

Everyone calmed down and we all stared at a massive German-owned container ship rising, ever so slowly, in the lock. Streams of water gushed from its nether regions while men in orange high-visibility jackets checked everything was going smoothly. A loudspeaker began to give a running commentary in Spanish and English, about where the boat had come from and where it was going. But what everyone wanted to hear was how much the ship's owners had paid to allow its passage through the canal. Eventually we found out. This one, we heard, cost $135,000.

"Expensive," I said, enjoying myself after all. Even though the ship was passing through at less than a walking pace, it was actually quite dramatic. The white egrets and grey pelicans swooping about the place helped too. As did the size of the ship – it was massive.

"Well it sounds expensive," said John, "but it's actually good value for the ship owner. The time and money they save by not having to navigate all the way around South America is well worth the cost."

I asked John how the canal authorities calculated the price.

"The tolls are based mainly on how big the ships are and how much cargo they can carry. But for cruise ships, it's a bit different. They pay for the number of passengers they have on board. The most expensive crossing was in 2010 when a Norwegian cruise ship paid $375,000 to pass through. The cheapest ever crossing was thirty-six cents. A man called Richard Halliburton swam the length of it in the 1920s, and when he finished, the authorities weighed him. That's how they calculated the cost."

After a while, the ship started moving onward towards the Atlantic Ocean, over fifty miles away, a journey that would take it about eight hours. Everyone strained their necks to see the next ship coming through. The whole process seemed laborious and time-consuming.

"What's the waiting period before a ship can get into the canal?" Angela asked John.

"It depends. During peak times, it can take up to a week. But if they want, they can pay a congestion charge and jump the queue. It costs a lot though. I know one ship that paid nearly a quarter of a million dollars to push in front of ninety other ships. Its normal fee was going to be something like $13,000, so the owners must have been desperate to bump it up."

Another ship was approaching the locks, a large Indian-registered one. After ten minutes, the new arrival began its ponderous ascent up through the Miraflores Locks, going through exactly the same process as the German ship, and I grew a little bored. One ship was enough for me, and I could tell Angela was getting restless too.

"Okay," John said. "I'll take you to the cinema so you can watch a movie on how the canal was made."

6

Despite my reservations, the short 15-minute film turned out to be interesting. We learned that in 1881, the designer of the Suez Canal, a Frenchman called Ferdinand de Lesseps, had started the mighty waterway. A few years into construction, he probably wished he hadn't bothered with the plan. Hundreds of his men were dying each month, due to a mixture of malaria, yellow fever and accidents. The Panamanian mountains also proved a tricky obstacle, difficult to traverse and covered in thick, insect-ridden jungle. The never-ending tropical rain added an element of further misery, quickly rusting any iron equipment and adding water to fuel the mosquito-breeding ponds. Finally, after nine years of hard labour, the Frenchman admitted defeat and abandoned ship, selling construction rights (and all his remaining machinery) to the Americans. By the time Lesseps left Panama, 22,000 men had lost their lives.

One of the first things the Americans did was to buy off the Panamanian government. With the payoff, they established a canal zone, whereby the future canal, plus five miles on either side, would be classed as US territory, protected by United States troops.

That done, they enticed workers from the States, promising good wages and three meals a day. Skilled workers arrived in their droves. The American engineers also set about sanitising the area, almost eradicating the mosquitoes that had plagued the French. Still, it took the Americans another decade to finish the canal, but in 1914, it was finally unveiled: a shortcut between the Pacific and Atlantic Ocean.

The Americans kept control of the canal until 1979. After that, it became jointly owned by America and Panama. In 1999, control was passed solely to the Government of Panama, and since then, it has been a money-spinner for the country, earning around $4.5 billion per year. No wonder the Panamanians were building another, wider lock, to cater for the super container ships that could not fit through the original locks.

7

The Panama Canal Museum was full of model ships, model trains and model hoisting machines. It also contained rock samples and grainy black and white photos of the men who had toiled away on the project. Due to John's presence, we lingered around the displays longer than we would have liked, but after a suitable time of chin rubbing and thoughtful reading, we finished our tour of the Panama Canal by going upstairs to see a static display of creepy crawlies endemic to Panama. The giant cockroaches were particularly disgusting, about two inches in length, looking like they could survive a bashing with a heavy book. A gigantic thing called the Titan beetle was also nasty looking. It was about seven inches long and its mandibles, we read, were sharp enough to snap a pencil in half. The worst insect however was something called a Hawk Wasp, an ugly black thing with red wings. The one in the display was attacking a tarantula.

"That's a nasty wasp," said John who had noticed us staring at the terrible scene. "The female will stun a tarantula and then lay a single egg inside its body. Then it will drag the spider back to its nest and block off the entrance. The poor spider will come around not knowing what has happened. But deep inside its body, the egg is growing, and eventually a grub will hatch and begin eating the tarantula from the inside. After it has feasted and grown big enough it will burst through the spider's body like a scene from *Alien*."

"Yuck," said Angela grimacing. "That's disgusting. And you get these wasps here – in Panama?"

"Yeah. They have the second most painful sting in the insect world. They're pretty docile most of the time though."

8

After the fun of the canal, we drove towards the colonial heartland of Panama City, an area known as Casco Viejo. To get there we had to drive through the notorious El Chorrillo district, one of the red sectors, i.e. dangerous neighbourhoods of Panama's capital.

"At night you would not want to be here," said John, "because there would be a very high chance of being robbed or killed. Even during the day it's not good for tourists. If the locals see you, they will assume you have money and will want it."

So why the hell are we driving through it, I thought? Especially inside a van painted with lizards and the words Panama Trails on the sides. If there was a more touristy mini-van in town, I'd yet to see it. It might as well have said, *Hello everyone, we're tourists! Come and rob us because we're stupid.*

Everything looked normal and day-to-day, though. People were sitting in cafes, chatting animatedly; children in school uniform laughed and joked as we drove by. Fruit and vegetable stalls were everywhere, all of them busy with women perusing the offerings on display. But despite the apparent carefree nature of El Chorrillo's citizens, the area looked down at heel and in need of some care and attention. The pavements were cracked and many storefronts had rusted iron bars fronting them. Along some rundown side streets, young men were sitting around doing nothing in particular. Like many nations in Latin America, the difference between rich and poor was vast, and El Chorrillo was a prime example of that.

"It used to have a wall surrounding it," John told us as we drove further into El Chorrillo. "One way in, one way out. At seven o'clock at night, they would lock the gates. And you did not want to be locked on the wrong side of the wall, I can tell you."

A minute later, John slowed down. "See that graffiti over there?" He was pointing at an image of a US soldier that someone had drawn as a devil. I was very conscious of the fact we had almost come to a standstill in a bad part of town, but John seemed unconcerned. "Lots of this stuff exists because Americans are not popular in this part of the city. It was because of the US invasion of Panama in 1989."

I remembered hearing about the invasion on the news, but as I was a teenager in the UK, it had barely registered. Basically, from what I could recall, the Americans had invaded the country to oust a wayward Panamanian president, but in the process, they had killed hundreds of Panamanian civilians caught up in the fighting.

"Yeah. That's basically it," John said, moving off again. "George Bush wanted to get rid of General Noriega because he thought he was threatening the running of the canal. Thousands of US troops came to Panama, and a lot of fighting happened here in El Chorrillo – because that's where the Panamanian force's headquarters were. After a month, the Americans won, and they captured General Noriega. But five hundred Panamanians died, quite a lot of them civilians from El Chorrillo. For that reason, the people who live here have never forgiven the Americans."

"What happened to the general?" I asked.

"He was taken to the States to stand trial. He ended up in prison there. But he's back in Panama now. The Panamanian authorities extradited him in 2011. He's currently in Renacer Prison."

We passed through El Chorrillo without mishap, and arrived into an area of narrow streets clogged with traffic. The cause of the jam was restoration work. Men were toiling away, laying new cobblestones, or adding concrete to cracked pavements. Casco Viejo, Panama's old town, was going to look amazing when it was finished.

Panama City, we found out, was almost five hundred years old. The Spanish founded it in 1519, when it became their base for expeditions into South America. As such, Panama City became one of the most important trading posts in the world, with Inca silver and gold passing through in great and shiny quantities. Unsurprisingly, Panama City attracted the attention of pirates, most notably Henry Morgan, who came to Panama in the late 17th century.

Captain Morgan was an English pirate, trained by the Royal Navy, who made his money raiding Spanish galleons and ports. With his band of privateers, he set his sights upon Panama City, but the Spanish thwarted his efforts because they found out about his impending attack and managed to hide most of their treasure on offshore ships. So maddened by this was Morgan that he ordered the destruction of Panama City, and soon the whole place was ablaze. Thousands died and the city had to be rebuilt on a different site.

Despite the poor takings, Morgan returned to England and was knighted by King Charles II for his services against the Spanish. The following year, he was made governor of Jamaica. Not only that: he ended up having a brand of rum named after him.

Baton-waving police officers directed the traffic through the old town until we eventually found a parking space. We climbed out and felt the heat immediately. I could only imagine how terrible it must have been for those early French construction workers toiling over the canal, especially with mosquitoes and leeches swarming over them.

Casco Viejo was definitely the prettiest part of Panama City. Old colonial buildings and attractive plazas were all around us, and in the distance, across the bay, were the skyscrapers. John led us past one set of fetching buildings – all pastel coloured, with pretty balconies filled with green pot plants – towards our first stop,

Iglesias de la Merced (Church of Our Lady of Mercy). The outside was nondescript, but that didn't matter; it was the inside that drew the crowds. We entered the church and then stared straight ahead. The golden altar glittered and shimmered. It was huge, featuring ornaments, statues, decorations and plinths.

"When Captain Morgan came," John told us, "he heard about this golden altar. When the priest found out that the pirate was on his way, he covered the altar in mud. Morgan arrived and saw only a dull altar, and asked the priest where the golden one was. The priest told him that some other pirates had already stolen it. Morgan believed him and actually gave a donation so the priest could buy a new altar."

We headed towards a central square called Plaza de la Independencia, where the founding fathers of Panama had once gathered in 1903 to declare their independence from Colombia. Apart from a few statues of the men, the square was now occupied by trinket stalls. Women wearing traditional costume tried to cajole Angela into buying some carvings made from large nuts, or necklaces filled with colourful beads. We managed to bypass them until we arrived at a small bar.

10

"I really like Panama," said Angela after she'd taken a sip of her drink. "I think I could live here." I nodded in agreement. The Atlas Beer I was drinking definitely hit the spot on such a hot and humid day.

"Yeah, it's a great place to live," added John, "and it's safe too. A lot of people imagine the worst about Latin America, but as long as you don't flash your dollars, or wave an expensive camera around, you'll be fine. The only exceptions are the red sectors, places like El Chorrillo. Tourists, or white people in general, need to stay out of them. The locals there will murder you for nothing." John looked wistful for a moment, seemingly lost in his own thoughts. "My wife and I had a man who trimmed our hedge a while back. For a few dollars, he'd show up with his hedge trimmer to keep the grass down in our back yard. He did most of the street too. One day he didn't show up. Later we found out he'd been walking home through El Chorrillo when a couple of men stopped him. They took his trimmer, his phone and twenty bucks. Then they shot him dead."

I looked at Angela. She looked a dumbfounded as me. We didn't know what to say and so said nothing.

"So yeah, Panama City is safe," said John, "But only as long as you keep to the right areas."

11

After finishing our drinks, we set off again, and I asked John whether he knew of anywhere I could buy a hat. I could feel the sun burning the top of my scalp and wanted to get it covered up before it got much worse.

"What sort of hat?"

"Just a normal, cap-type thing. I've left mine at the hotel."

John nodded. "What about a Panama hat?"

I thought for moment. Would I suit a Panama hat? Was I of the right age to pull it off? I wasn't sure. I asked Angela what she thought.

"I think you should buy one," she told me. "A Panama hat bought in Panama City – what could be better?"

John led us to an outdoor stall that sold just Panama hats. They were laid out across two large tables and I didn't know which one to pick. The man in charge decided to help me out.

"These here," he said, pointing at a whole bunch of hats, "are the cheapest. Six dollars each. But look." He picked one up and turned it upside down. "The lining is very...how you say...scratchy. And the stitching is not so good." He led me to another section of his extensive stall. "These are twenty dollars each. Good quality hat. Okay for you, I think." He passed me it to feel. It was clearly better than the budget hat. "But these ones over here," continued the man, "are the best of all. One hundred dollars each. But look." He picked one up and rolled it into a tight tube. When he released it, the hat immediately sprang back into shape. There was not a crease to be seen anywhere. "Only the hundred dollar hat will do this," the man said. "So it's up to you."

I chose the medium-range one, and handed over twenty dollars. After putting it on, John and Angela nodded appreciatively, and so did the hat seller.

12

We finished our tour of Casco Viejo by wandering to the old French Quarter. Even though the French had failed at constructing a canal, they had succeeded in building a nice square overlooking the ocean. A couple of other tourists were there already, taking pictures of each other; when they noticed us, both stared at my hat. Whether they thought I looked ridiculous or not, I couldn't tell. After nodding at them, we walked to a railing overlooking the ocean. The long line of gleaming skyscrapers in the distance seemed to be shimmering in the heat. Further off, anchored in the Pacific Ocean, were a group of ships, all of them waiting to pass through the famous canal.

In the middle of the square was a large obelisk with a rooster on top. The rooster was the symbol of France, and the monument was dedicated to the thousands of French construction workers who had died building the Panama Canal. Underneath was a series of vaults containing an art gallery and a restaurant. During colonial times, the vaults had been prison cells. Because of their low-level position, the incoming tide often flooded them. "Sometimes," explained John, "prisoners were chained up outside the dungeons and left there to drown."

"Nice," I said.

After a wander through another craft market, we made our way back to the car. "Okay, you have two choices now," said John. "I can either drive you guys back to your hotel, or I can take you to the Causeway. The Causeway is a long stretch of road linking four different islands. You'll find plenty of restaurants and shops there. Plus, you'll easily be able to get a cab back to your hotel, or wherever else you want to go. It's up to you."

We decided on the Causeway.

The palm-fringed Causeway was decidedly nice, flanked by ocean on both sides. Small sailing boats sloshed about in the water and pelicans dipped and dived for fish around them. Just behind the line of restaurants was a small, but deliciously tropical beach – all palm trees, white sand and azure ocean. A few people sat sunbathing on it. After saying goodbye to John, we chose a restaurant and sat down.

"What shall we do this afternoon?" asked Angela. Our meals had just arrived, a delicious blend of local fish and rice.

"I think we should go to the rainforest."

"Good idea."

Thirty minutes later, I picked up my new hat and sunglasses. It was time to flag a taxi down.

13

The taxi to the rainforest only took ten minutes because the Metropolitan Natural Park was inside the city limits of the capital. We paid the entrance fee and set off on a jungle trail that supposedly offered sloths, anteaters and terrapins.

The terrapins were easy to spot because they were all in one place – loitering around a large pond just near the entrance. About ten of them were basking in the sun, heads turned up into the air, while the rest sat dunked in the water. As we approached, most of the sunbathers dived into the pond, but one big specimen remained, its reptilian eyes staring, as if daring us to approach. We moved on, passing through thick forest, twisting vines, bulging wasps' nests and a constant cacophony of insect noises. It felt like we were in a Tarzan movie.

"Where do sloths live?" I asked Angela. I imagined it was up in the trees, but couldn't be totally sure.

"I don't know," admitted my wife as we both stared upwards towards the canopy. "But it must be up there."

I nodded, scanning the trees.

Occasionally, a bright blue butterfly would tumble past or a vivid red bird would fly across our path, but the sloths, at least so far, were keeping themselves well hidden.

We walked on, finding that the trail was heading upwards into denser rainforest. It really was amazing that such a place existed within Panama City, and I was glad the city builders had had the forethought to keep it. But the humidity was horrendous. Even after just twenty minutes, I looked like a wreck.

"Look," said Angela, pointing to the ground. It was a line of leaf-cutter ants. They were all diligently trooping over a fallen log, and then crossing the path we were walking on. There were thousands of them, half their number carrying carefully cut sections of green leaf towards the nest, the other half walking in the opposite direction to get more leaves. Some looked like they were carrying green hang gliders on their backs. It was amazing to watch and we were careful to step over the ant caravan as we made our way uphill.

"By the way," Angela said. "I think you look a bit of an idiot in that Panama hat."

I was taken aback. I stopped and faced my wife. "I beg your pardon? An idiot? If I recall correctly, it was you who said I should buy it in the first place. I spent twenty dollars on it!"

Angela laughed. "It just doesn't go. You look...*wrong* in it."

We walked on in silence. My hat was staying on, for the time being at least.

"Stupid bloody sloths," I said. "Where the hell are they? Aren't they supposed to be lazy animals, doing nothing all day?"

Both of us stopped to scan some branches again. No sign of a sloth anywhere. Maybe they were really high up, right up in the tree tops, but after craning our necks towards the canopy, we gave up and trudged onwards. Just then, we heard a rustling sound. It was coming from up ahead, around a jungle bend. Cautiously we moved forward, fully expecting a jaguar to attack or a sloth to appear, but were disappointed to find a young couple climbing down a steep trail.

"Hi," the woman said, in an American accent. Her boyfriend smiled.

"Hi," Angela replied.

In turn, I smiled, tipping my Panama hat at them.

The woman regarded it but said nothing.

"There's a good view from up there," her companion said. "Just follow the trail around to the top and you'll see."

"Did you see a sloth up there?" I asked hopefully.

"A sloth? No, not yet," the woman said. "But hey, fingers crossed."

As they walked past us, we headed upwards, crashing through branches and sending insects scattering in all directions. At the top, we found a small platform with a fence around its perimeter. Below, in the distance, were the skyscrapers of Panama City again. From up here, it was possible to see just how expansive the city actually was.

"Sloth, sloth, where are you?" I called into the trees. "Coming ready or not."

Angela told me to stop being so stupid. "It's probably because of you that we're not seeing any sloths. You're too noisy."

I walked over to a tree and stared upwards. There was nothing in it apart from dense foliage and creepy crawlies. I tried to shake it but it was far too sturdy for me to move it even one millimetre. Sighing heavily, I joined Angela at the fence.

"What would you do?" I said, "if we got back to where that couple were, and we saw them lying on the ground, dead, with a couple of sloths eating them?"

Angela didn't answer. A few minutes later, we were heading back down the hill, resigned to not seeing a sloth. We followed a signpost that pointed towards the exit.

And then we saw one.

The furry creature was a beige-coloured thing, about the same size as a small dog, and it was slothing about in a mid-level branch just metres away from the finish line. Silently we crept up to the mammal and stared up at it. It didn't move a muscle, but we could see the three toes of its arms curled around a couple of branches. Like all sloths, it was fast asleep.

At first, we whispered, not wanting to startle the creature, but after a few moments of this, we began clicking and purring, trying to cajole the sloth from its slumber. It was to no avail, though; there was no waking the little animal. I considered throwing a piece of fruit at it, or poking it with a long stick, but Angela wouldn't entertain that idea.

"Wake up!" I bellowed through cupped hands. "Wakey wakey!"

"Stop it," snapped Angela. "Leave it alone."

After waiting a minute more, hoping it would move, we finally admitted defeat and moved away. Nevertheless, both of us left the park happy at seeing one of the elusive creatures in the middle of Panama City.

15

"So that's Panama done," I said at the hotel. We'd just returned from an evening meal at a restaurant opposite the nearby casinos.

Angela was folding some clothes in preparation for the suitcase. "Yeah, and I really liked it."

"I did too," I was packing some of my things, though not as diligently as my wife was doing. My tried and tested way of packing a suitcase was to throw everything in and press down hard. If the lid closed afterwards, then it was a job done well. It was a method that infuriated Angela, but it was one that I had perfected over time, and so far, it had never failed me.

"What are you going to do with your Panama hat?"

"Keep it of course. And wear it with pride."

Angela shook her head. "You're joking, right? You know you look stupid in it. It's embarrassing, actually."

"I don't care."

"Yes, you do."

"I don't. Besides, if it annoys you, all the better."

Angela smiled but said nothing. I picked up the hat and put it on my head. At the wardrobe mirror, I regarded myself. I did look like an idiot, but kept that thought to myself. "Yeah, looking good," I said, tipping it this way and that. "Dapper and sophisticated. A proper traveller. I might buy myself a monocle."

I removed the hat and carefully folded it up and returned it to my suitcase. Gently, I pushed it into the corner and closed the lid. After some hefty one-armed pushing, I managed to zip the thing up. Satisfied, I cracked open a cold beer from the fridge. "Done," I announced. "In a tenth of the time it takes you."

I checked our flight details for the following morning. Our next journey would take us southwards, crossing over the Equator to the Southern Hemisphere. The capital of Peru was our next stop on the adventure. It was time to leave Central America and head to South America proper.

Top row: A huge ship passing through the Panama Canal;
Angela and me in Panama City
Middle row: Twisty skyscraper that almost cost me my
marriage; Street scene of Panama City; Expensive boats along the
Causeway
Bottom row: Me, sporting the $20 Panama hat; Downtown
Panama City

Chapter 2. Deepest, Darkest Peru

Interesting Fact: It never rains in Lima.

The Panamanian Airlines flight landed at Lima's Jorge Chavos International with a round of applause. Why this happened in some countries and not others was still a mystery to Angela and me, but whatever the reason, the airliner taxied us to the very modern-looking terminal.

Our stay in the Peruvian capital was going to be a brief one. Like most people who visited Peru, Lima was merely a gateway to places like Cusco or Lake Titicaca, both of which we would be visiting later. One evening in Lima was all the time we had and so we endeavoured to make the most of it.

"When my brother came here a few years ago," Angela told me as we jumped in the back of a taxi, "he said it was a bit of a dump." As we left the airport, I quickly began to concur. The weather didn't help. A grey mist hung in the air, obscuring the sun and casting dismal shadows over the sorry-looking buildings beyond the airport perimeter. Mind you, it was winter in South America.

"The sky is like this for eight months of the year," said the taxi driver who had noticed us staring up at the gloom. "Only in the summer will we see the sun. But at least it never rains in Lima."

"Really?" I said, not quite believing this statement.

"Yes. Look at the roads. There are no drains. Lima does not need them. We get all our water from the mountains."

2

Lima has a population of about nine million, making it one of the largest cities in the world. The Peruvian capital has more people living in it than London, Hong Kong and Chicago. This, of course, brings with it the usual problems of congestion and pollution. The road we were on was thick with traffic.

Many vehicles had dents and scratches, and about half had some sort of rust filler applied. The traffic was the usual mix of minivans, taxis, rust bucket cars, and bizarrely, red tuk-tuks – the three-wheeled vehicles more commonly seen in Asia. The buildings by the side looked tired and in need of a good lick of paint. Lima looked like a functioning, working city but not a very pretty one.

We joined a busy highway, flanked with billboards advertising everything from Samsung and Volkswagen, to a Canadian branch of Scotiabank. A man pushing a cartload of wooden bed frames was causing a nuisance in the road, especially as he was hogging the two middle lanes of the four-lane highway. Suddenly, the car in front braked heavily, ridiculously so in the slow-moving traffic. We came to an abrupt stop.

"Student driver," said our taxi driver by way of explanation. On the back of the student's car was a large white sticker saying *vehiculo de instruccion.*

"Lima has a lot of people," said our driver, as we passed a white minivan stuffed with locals. The driver's arm was dangling over the side of the open window, a cigarette in his hand. "And one of the reasons we have so many people is because they have moved here from the provinces. They do this for safety. Have you heard of the Shining Path?"

I nodded. The Shining Path was a communist organisation. Through violence and intimidation, they had gained control of vast areas of the Peruvian countryside. Their heyday was in the 1980s, when Shining Path guerrillas had carried out massacres and set up labour camps for those who opposed them. To escape the onslaught, peasants flocked to the capital and had remained ever since. This was despite the fact that the leader of the organisation, a former university lecturer by the name of Abimael Guzmanhad was caught in 1992.

"People are still worried," said the driver, lighting a cigarette. "Things can change quickly in Peru."

Our hotel stood on the high ground of Miraflores, one of the nicer parts of Lima. It was an area full of skyscrapers, bars, restaurants and a large shopping mall called Larcomar. Our driver pointed out the ocean, a grey cauldron of foamy water topped with a thick layer of cloud. "The Pacific looks cold today. Not good for swimming, I think. But this area, Miraflores, means 'see the flowers,' of which you will see many. You will also see that your hotel has beautiful ocean views, and this whole district is perfectly safe, day or night."

After checking in, we wasted no time in having a wander around. The ocean was still full of stormy waves, braved only by a few hardy surfers and a couple of insane paragliders. The sky was a lighter shade of grey and, despite what the man had said earlier, it looked like it was going to pour down.

"Why aren't you wearing your Panama hat?" asked Angela.

"Because it's not sunny. But don't you worry. It'll be back in business soon."

"Lima is grim," Angela said as we walked inland to the centre of Miraflores. "And this is the nicest bit. My brother was right."

The street we were on was Avenue Jose Larco, a long thoroughfare filled with shops, banks and casinos. We wandered along with the crowds, staring into what Angela described as 1970s shops – all glass-fronted displays full of shoes and boots. There were plenty of Peruvian flags about though, a standard red and white tricolour, because by chance our arrival into the country had coincided with the impending independence celebrations.

Peru's history goes hand in hand with the Incas, an empire that lasted less than a hundred years. Its timeline ran between 1438 and 1532. When I found this out, I was surprised. I'd always thought that the Incas were in the same period as the Ancient Greeks, or even the Romans, a civilisation from thousands of years ago and one that had lasted for centuries. A hundred years? That didn't sound like long.

We found a bar and ordered some drinks. When they arrived, I turned to Angela. "Did you know that the Incas were around only five hundred years ago – the same time as Henry VIII?"

"Yes."

"Really?"

"Well I didn't know they were around the same time as Henry VIII, but I knew they were around fairly recently."

"How did you know?" I picked up my bottle of beer and took a sip. Even though we were in the middle of a Peruvian winter, it was warm enough to sit outside at a bar. And now that the sun was going down, and the lights were coming on, Lima was looking a little more welcoming.

"Because I'm clever."

I nodded. "Okay then: why did the Inca Empire decline, Miss Clever Clogs?"

"Because of the Spanish. When the Spanish found out about the silver in Peru, they came to steal it. And in return, they infected the Incas with smallpox. It killed lots of them."

I looked at my wife closely. She looked back and then picked up her drink. I nodded thoughtfully. "How do you know all this?"

"Because I'm clever," she repeated. "Actually, I just read it in the guidebook while you went to the toilet."

4

"It reminds me of Bulgaria," said Angela. We were passing yet another 1970s-style shopping arcade. I knew what she meant. Lima was a bit ragged around the edges but it had more or less everything you might need. A few cracked pavements here, a black-stained building there, but a KFC if the desire took you.

"That building looks nice," I said. We were in the middle of a busy shopping street thronging with people. Some young backpackers were walking in front of us, maps in hand, large bags strapped tightly to their backs. The building was a pleasing yellow colour with a nice large wooden door. It turned out to be an art gallery.

Ignoring the art, we found another bar near Kennedy Park, a small fenced-off area full of stray cats. People were clearly looking after the cats, however, because none appeared skinny or wary of humans. Later we found out the park's nickname was, in fact, Cat Park. As I sipped my Cristal Beer, I looked at Angela and said my favourite Spanish phrase again, the one where I'm asking for a beer.

"Oh, stop it, will you," sighed Angela. "You sound like a bandit from a Clint Eastwood film."

"Una cervesa para usted, si?" I asked in the thickest accent I could muster.

Angela shot me a glance. "What does that mean?"

"It means, a beer for you, yes?"

"No, but I'll have another glass of wine, please." I looked around and attracted the attention of a waiter. Angela noticed the smile on my face. "Please don't," she said. "It'll be embarrassing."

"Hola, senor," I said with a flourish. "Una cervesa para mi, y un vino blanco, por favor."

The waiter nodded and walked away.

"See," I said. "I'm an expert."

5

As we walked back to the hotel, both of us agreed that we'd been a little harsh on the Peruvian capital. Miraflores had some nice bits, and unlike what we'd expected, the streets had been safe and pleasant. After stopping to grab a pizza, we made our way to the hotel to begin our packing.

"I wonder how we'll cope with the altitude in Cusco." I said. Cusco was 3400 metres above sea level, which is 11,200 feet.

Sickness was a major problem for many tourists when they first arrived in the city. From the information I'd read, the best thing to do was to take it easy for the first few days, but with only four days in Cusco, Angela and I would have little time for that, especially when we had to see Machu Picchu as well.

"What are the symptoms?" asked Angela.

"Headaches, feeling tired, stomach ache and shortness of breath."

"That doesn't sound too bad."

"No, but they can lead to double vision and coughing up a pink frothy liquid. And also irrational behaviour – but you have that already."

"Funny."

"We'll just have to keep an eye out."

Top row: Street scene of downtown Lima; Miraflores district
Middle row: The dramatic coastline of Miraflores; On approach to
the airport
Bottom row: Me enjoying a local beer; The airport road

Chapter 3. Cusco, the gateway to Machu Picchu

Interesting fact: Potatoes, tomatoes and avocados originated in Peru.

Instead of enduring a 21-hour road journey from Lima to Cusco, Angela and I boarded a Lan Peru airliner that only took one hour. After the gloom and greyness of Lima, Cusco turned out to be a welcome change, with blue sky, bright sun and an imposing mountainous backdrop to boot. And there was the promise of a trip to Machu Picchu later that week. Unless altitude sickness got to us first.

Breathing was difficult from the outset. Being at an altitude of over eleven thousand feet meant we had to slow our normal walking pace and stop for constant breathers. After only a block or two of wandering the picture-postcard cobbled streets of downtown Cusco, we were breathing heavily, straining to get enough oxygen to our lungs. My chest was heaving and I wondered how we would cope being so high up for the next week or so. And we still had La Paz in Bolivia to go! That was even higher than Cusco.

"How are you doing?" I asked Angela.

Angela gulped a large lungful of air. "It's definitely hard going. Apart from that, I seem okay."

Everywhere we looked was so pretty, though. Old women with long braided hair and top hats wandered up and down the streets, some with trinkets laid over their arms, others carrying large bags on their backs. Stray dogs slept in the shade or trotted around looking for food, but all of them seemed friendly and non-threatening. Men laughed and joked with each other, and we heard the sound of music: trumpets and drums. It was coming from a nearby building. When we passed its doors we saw people dancing.

Angela and I arrived at the large and beautiful Plaza de Armas, the central and busiest part of Cusco, and the most photographed.

The square was dominated by not one church, but two. One was Cusco Cathedral, the other the Church of Jesus. Both looked magnificent, built by the Spanish on the sites of former Inca temples.

Following an unsuccessful rebellion in 1780, the Spanish carried out one of their most gruesome executions in Plaza de Armas. The rebel leader, Tupac Amaru II was forced to watch as the Spanish executed his wife and then his son. Afterwards, he became centre stage when they cut off his tongue and tied his hands and feet to four different horses, with him suspended in the centre. The horses were pointing at each corner of the square, and then the order was given for them to charge, which they did, ripping Amaru's arms and legs off, a process known as quartering. The Spanish then picked up the bloody torso, chopped the head off, and placed it on a spike. Today, instead of spikes and bloody puddles, the centre of the square was a place of fountains, pigeons and a golden statue of an Inca warrior.

Angela and I found a bench to sit on so we could catch our breath. Though we'd barely walked a couple of kilometres, it felt like we had run a marathon.

2

The Incas had constructed Cusco in the shape of a puma, erecting temples, palaces and all manner of grand buildings. But after the Spanish took over, they destroyed the Inca temples and made Cusco their base for colonisation of other parts of South America. But the Spanish had made some great buildings too.

"Everywhere I look is so picturesque," said Angela as we swept our gaze around the square. As well as the churches, there were bars and cafes, as well as endless souvenir shops. Up in the hills were simple dwellings, filling the mountainsides until they thinned due to the gradient, leaving only bare, brown earth. On one large patch of mountain, the words Viva le Peru had been carved: a fitting backdrop to the city of Cusco.

The square was popular with local families, quite often with young children chasing the many pigeons that fluttered around and about. Suitably rested, Angela and I walked west from the square, avoiding the men trying to flog us paintings and the young women trying to sell massages.

We arrived at Cusco Central Market, a bustling indoor place of clothes, fruit and vegetables, and eatery sections where locals were chomping away on bowls of chicken and pork. In another section, deeper inside the market, pigs' heads, lolling tongues, red and white innards, and cow faces were all on offer. So were dangling spheres of flesh that we could only assume were testicles. In a dark alcove, we passed a bucket full of frogs, all of them waiting to be cooked in a large soup pot.

An old woman was sitting on the floor next to piles of cheese. She was knitting to pass the time, but glanced up briefly as we walked by her impromptu stall. "Oh my God," whispered Angela. "Look over there." I looked and immediately saw what she was referring to. A pile of horse lips were smiling dementedly at us. We were so shocked that we did a double pass of the terrible pile, just to make sure our eyes were not deceiving us. We left the market in need of fresh air.

3

"Well, do you know what? I love Cusco," Angela announced as we found somewhere for lunch. "It's much better than I expected – and I was expecting a lot. Lima doesn't even compare."

We found a restaurant on the edge of the main square. Its extensive menu was written in four different languages, every meal with an accompanying photograph, which to me, is never a good sign. Expensive, high-quality restaurants never show photos of their food, and neither do they have a menu with a hundred different meals on offer.

"It's got cuy," I said, pointing at the picture of a fried guinea pig with chips. Its head and paws were clearly shown, making it look distinctly unappetising. I could only imagine the reaction of a British schoolchild at seeing their cute furry pet stripped of its skin and fried on a long skewer.

"Horrible."

"I know. That's why I'm going to get one."

Angela's eyes shot open. "You're not?"

"Yep. I've tried horse in Kazakhstan, bear in Estonia and whale in Iceland. And now I'm going to try guinea pig in Peru."

When the waiter came over, Angela ordered some tomato soup, the only thing she felt like eating. The altitude sickness was starting to affect her appetite. And mine too, though not as badly. With Angela watching me, I decided against the guinea pig (it was far too expensive for something I would probably only take one bite of), and ordered some steak and chips instead. Fried guinea pig would have to wait for another day.

Angela's tomato soup turned out to be warm water with a dollop of tomato ketchup mixed in. It looked disgusting and tasted worse. Angela put her spoon down and deemed the broth inedible. "I can't believe they serve that as tomato soup," she said. "It's the worst soup I've ever had."

My food was acceptable, but only just. But the warning signs had been there from the start: the extensive menu, the photos, and the distinct lack of people. The only thing the place had going for it was its cheapness. We left, vowing never to return.

4

Cusco by night was just as visually appealing. The two churches were atmospherically lit in a pleasing yellow glow, and the hubbub of people could be heard over the sound of car tyres clattering over the cobbled streets. The bars around the edge of the square were particularly busy. One of them was called Paddy's Pub, and claimed to be the *Highest 100% Irish Owned Pub on the planet*.

At the top of some rickety steps, we entered the packed bar. It was full of western tourists, most of them young backpacker types. After ordering a pint of Guinness for me and a wine for Angela, we relocated to one of Paddy's Pub's outdoor balconies. In the distance, we could see twinkling lights on the hillsides surrounding Cusco.

Nearby was a young man holding court with two young women. He looked like he'd been on the road for a while, and from what we could gather, he'd only just met the two girls, and was now in the process of imparting his vast knowledge onto them.

"Yeah," he said, in a slow, but well-educated British accent. "I've travelled all the way down Central America to get here. Nine months now. I've seen some amazing places – like Tikal in Guatemala, and Bay Islands in Honduras. You know that place?"

The girls shook their heads, hanging from his every word.

"It's got some of the best snorkelling in the world there – a huge reef. And they play reggae music on the beach. I adored it. You should go there if you get the chance."

The girls, who judging by their accents, were Irish, told their new pal that they had had a bit of a nasty experience in Lima. Someone had tried to snatch one of their bags.

"Sorry to hear that," Mr Brit said, "but Belize is worse than Lima, believe me. I was in Belize City about a month ago. I'd just arrived and had just climbed off a bus. It was late evening and getting a bit dark and as I put my backpack on, I noticed this guy following me. He looked like he'd been living rough, and I just knew he was up to no good – you get a feeling for things like that after a while – and it didn't surprise me when he made a move. He ran up to me and tried to unzip the top part of my bag, but I pushed him away. He ran off a few feet and then picked up a rock. If I hadn't ducked, he'd have got me with it, but the rock hit a parked taxi. It bounced off the window."

"Wow," said one of the girls. "That's bad."

"Yeah, and then the next thing I knew, this huge, fat taxi driver jumped out of his car and opened his boot. He had a machete in there. I'm not joking, a machete!"

The girls shook their heads and looked at the man in open astonishment.

"The homeless guy was already running away; I think he'd seen the machete. The taxi driver ran past me, chasing after him. It was like something from a film. They disappeared down an alleyway and it must have been a dead end 'cause all I could see was a shadow of a man hacking at another man. Up and down his arm went. Up and down. The screaming was terrible. I turned around and ran. I couldn't believe what I'd just seen. It made me feel sick."

I looked at Angela. She looked sick too.

5

The next morning, we were up with the sun for our day trip to the Lost Site of the Incas. Unlike all the backpackers in Cusco, Angela and I were going by train. The thought of three nights of camping and trekking along the Inca Trail sounded like pure torment to us. Besides, with only a few days in Peru, we didn't have time.

"Jesus," I whimpered, "this lack of oxygen is really getting to me." I was wheezing like an asthmatic and every step seemed like I'd climbed a staircase.

"How's your head?"

"Not as bad as last night."

For both of us, the previous night had been a fitful one. Broken sleep and gulping for air like fish were the classic symptoms of mild altitude sickness. But the headaches were the worst thing. Mine seemed to permeate my entire skull, compounding my misery as I tried to sleep. But at least we hadn't suffered as badly as one woman in our hotel. Over breakfast, we found out that she ended up needing the hotel's emergency oxygen mask, a feature of most tourist establishments in Cusco. After a few minutes of precious O_2, she was taken to a nearby clinic.

The organisers of the Machu Picchu daytrip had a well-oiled machine on their hands. A guide took us to Poroy Station, twenty minutes from the centre of Cusco, where we congregated with our fellow passengers. Almost all of them were wearing sturdy hiking boots, thick puffer jackets and expensive waterproof jackets. I stood shivering in my T-shirt while Angela huddled next to me in her open-toed sandals.

"I hope we're not hiking up the bloody thing?" I whispered to Angela. I spied a coffee machine; the coffee was horrible, but at least it was hot. We relocated to the side of the room to wait for the boarding announcement. Fifteen minutes later, it came, and we all trooped aboard the blue Perurail carriages for a three-an-a-half-hour journey to Machu Picchu. Angela and I sat down opposite a sixty-something couple, who told us they were from Belgium. Margot and Thomas were both retired teachers. Peru was their first trip outside of Europe.

6

"We have always taken our holidays in neighbouring countries," said Margot, who seemed the more talkative. "Places we can drive to, such as Germany, France and Italy. But with the children long gone, and more time on our hands, we decided to go somewhere different. So we're in Peru!"

"Wow," I said. "A big step then."

Thomas nodded but elected to remain mute. He turned to look outside at the scenery we were passing. It was a rural landscape of brown and yellow hills mixed with farmland. In the distance were some jagged mountains, all of them covered with snow.

"Yes, but our daughter is already here in Peru," said Margot. "That is why we're here really. She is hiking the trail with three of her friends, and we are, hopefully, going to meet up with her today sometime."

As the journey progressed, Margot's husband became more talkative. He was interested in all the places we had been to, especially some of the places in Asia.

"You two seem so brave," Thomas told us, "going to all these different places. And do you want to know something funny? For thirty years I was a geography teacher and the furthest I travelled was Rome."

"We're not brave," said Angela. "We're just lucky that we've been able to do what we do."

"Look at that!" said Margot excitedly. Outside was a field with a few llamas munching on grass.

"My God," said Thomas, equally as thrilled. "Are they really llamas?"

Angela and I glanced at each other. Margot and Thomas were enthused by everything. Every time we passed a gushing river or a simple homestead, they would widen their eyes and tell us they had never seen anything like it.

"This is amazing," Margot said as we passed through another mountain village. "Everything is so different, so new."

They were right. But for Angela and me it was not *that* new. Sure, we had not seen this particular area of countryside before, and had never experienced sitting inside a Perurail carriage, but we had done similar things in other countries. I envied Thomas and Margot – their fresh eyes experiencing something brand new. For them, Peru was a magical time, one of high adventure and full to the brim with mesmerising sights. To Angela and me, it was just another country along the way, albeit an exciting one.

I remembered going on holiday as a child and being so excited that I could barely sleep the night before. When my family drove to somewhere in England, usually a caravan park by the coast, I used to sit in the back of the car with my younger brothers, marvelling at going on *holiday*! And the first few times I flew in an aeroplane were magical, something almost unbelievable. I'd even look forward to the flight back home so I could experience the exhilaration again. But all that was in the past. Those initial feelings of pure, raw excitement had long gone. Somewhere along the line, Angela and I had become so used to visiting new places and flying on so many airliners that holidays had turned almost normal, perhaps even mundane. Had Angela and I become jaded travellers, I speculated? I hoped not, but seeing Thomas's and Margot's open-eyed astonishment at travelling by train through Peru did make me wonder.

"I didn't realise the rural parts of Peru would be so poor," said Margot. We were passing another small village with animals wandering around untethered. Men were tending the fields with what looked like ancient implements. "We are so lucky to live in Europe, don't you think?"

"Yeah," Angela said wistfully. I wondered whether she was experiencing the same melancholy feelings as me. "I suppose we are."

"But then again," Margot continued, "at least there is no rain here. The rain back home is shocking. It really is. It is always raining in Belgium."

"Not as much as in England," I said.

"What do you mean?" laughed Thomas. "In the United Kingdom, you get a few heavy showers, whereas we Belgians get downpours. You Brits always moan about the weather, but compared to us, you live in the Sahara!"

Margot smiled. "He's right. It is always grey and dismal where we live. But there is a saying in Flanders: if we did not have the weather to discuss, then there would be nothing to talk about. Isn't that right, Thomas?"

Beneath our seats, the wheels of the Perurail carriage trundled onwards and upwards.

7

The train pulled into Machu Picchu train station within one minute of its stated arrival time, a pleasing way to start our tour. Very quickly, we were put into groups depending on whether we could speak English, Spanish or French. We said goodbye to our Belgian friends and joined a small group composed of a thirty-something married German couple and a twenty-something American couple. The Americans were from Los Angeles, and both possessed the highly toned bodies expected of those who lived in L.A. The Germans were from Hamburg, and looked like they enjoyed eating hamburgers.

We all boarded a bus and drove for twenty-five minutes up a zigzag trail with sheer drops. An affable Peruvian called Alfredo was in charge of our group, and when we'd parked at the top of the hill, he gathered us outside the bus to give a brief history of Machu Picchu. All around us were other tour groups, guides and coaches. The place was heaving.

"This Inca site is almost eight thousand feet above sea level," said Alfredo. "Most archaeologists believe it was built around 1450, but was then abandoned about a hundred years later. One possible reason is that the people died from smallpox, which, as you probably know, the Spanish brought over with them. But no one knows for sure whether this is right, especially since the Spanish never actually found Machu Picchu. Come, let's go see it."

Alfredo took us up to a spot where we could all gaze down at the Inca wonder. It was the place where a million photographs had already been taken, but we took a few more anyway. Our companions were doing the same thing. It was just how we'd imagined it would be – a mass of Inca ruins, interspersed with green, with a distinctive mountain backdrop behind it.

"You are lucky with the weather," said Alfredo. "Yesterday it rained a lot, and there was a mist hanging over the site." We regarded the blue sky and then the sun. Later, I would discover a red triangle of sunburn below my neck, but at that moment, Machu Picchu seemed the perfect temperature.

Alfredo produced a folded A4 photo of Machu Picchu from his pocket. After smoothing it out, he showed it to us. "Tell me what you see?" he asked.

We all peered at the photo and shrugged. It was Machu Picchu, of course. In fact, it looked like the photographer had been standing in the same place as us. The American girl told him it was Machu Picchu. Alfredo nodded and then rotated the photo by ninety degrees.

"What do you see now?"

The effect was extraordinary. The photo now showed a man's head, complete with nose, mouth, lips and chin.

"Good, isn't it?" Alfredo said.

8

An American gentleman called Hiram Bingham discovered Machu Picchu in 1911. He named it the Lost City of the Incas, and a few years later published his findings in National Geographic magazine. People read about his find and started to see it for themselves. Initially, it was only a few visitors per year, but then the drops became a trickle and the trickle became a flood.

The overflow of people got so bad that archaeologists warned the Peruvian government that if they didn't restrict the number of tourists visiting Machu Picchu, then untold damage would result. And then, they warned, no one would come and a major source of income for Peru would run dry. The authorities didn't like the sound of that and so from 2011, they decreed that only 2500 people a day could enter the site. But that was still a lot of people. We could see groups of them standing among the ruins or following guides along the trails. After admiring the view for a few moments longer, we headed down hill to join them.

For the next hour or so, Alfredo took us on a tour of all the important sections of Machu Picchu, including the Watchman's Hut, Sun Temple, Condor Temple and Royal Residence before taking us to another viewing platform favoured by lizards and red spiky plants. Below us, deep down in a canyon were some tiny train tracks running parallel to a river.

"In January 2010, that river burst its banks," said Alfredo. "It trapped nearly two thousand tourists up here. They had to be airlifted out." I remembered seeing it on the news. I peered at the river and noticed just how close it was to the railway tracks. Thankfully, there was no sign of rain.

9

Alfredo took the six of us back to where the coaches were. After checking some of his paperwork, he pointed to Angela and me. "You two have got lunch included in your ticket price. I'll take you there in a moment." He looked at the other four people. "I'm afraid you haven't. But you can always buy some yourself. It's up to you."

The LA couple looked unperturbed by the news, joyous even. "Don't worry," said the blonde babe. "We ate a slice of lettuce yesterday, and we have a bag of couscous hidden away for emergencies. Besides, we want to go hiking around here. Burn off some calories after eating a stick of celery for breakfast."

The Germans conferred for a moment and then decided to head straight back down the hill. After waving everyone off, we followed Alfredo into a nearby buffet-style restaurant. After sorting us out, he wished us well and went off to find his next tour group.

"How excited are you?" I asked Angela after we'd sat down with our meals. The choice of food available was not great, but there was lots of it.

She looked confused. "Excited? Right now, you mean?"

"Yes."

Angela scooped up a piece of what looked like chicken. "One out of ten. Having a meal isn't one of the most exciting things to do."

I nodded and ate a slice of beef. "Okay, how excited were you when you saw Machu Picchu?"

Angela thought for a moment. "Maybe five or six."

"Okay. How excited are you about going to Lake Titicaca in a few days' time?"

"Why are you asking these questions?"

I put my fork down. "I just wonder whether we're becoming blasé about all the things we see and do. Most people would put seeing Machu Picchu at an eight or a nine. But you gave it a six. I'd give it the same. Yes, it looked great; yes, I'm glad we've seen it; but things like that don't get our pulses racing anymore. Remember when we went to Japan? We were both really excited. And the first time we visited the souqs in Marrakech? We loved it. But seeing Machu Picchu – one of the New Seven Wonders of the World – all we could muster was a six out of ten. We weren't excited by it."

"I was," Angela cut in.

I looked outside at the lines of people queuing for the journey back down to the train station. We would be joining them soon.

"What's brought this on?" Angela asked.

"It was that Belgian couple on the train. They were excited at being in Peru: excited at being on holiday. We weren't as excited as they were, and I'm a little jealous of that, I suppose."

I picked up my bottle of Inca Kola, undecided whether I actually liked the Peruvian soft drink. Instead of being dark brown, it was a golden yellow. Its taste was unlike any other cola I'd tried, with a sort of vanilla essence to it.

Angela stared at me. She picked up her own Inca Kola and took a sip. "Look. I agree that we're not as starry-eyed as we used to be, but I'm still excited about Lake Titicaca and Rio de Janeiro. When I think of seeing a tango dance in Buenos Aires, *that* makes me excited. We're not blasé, Jason, we're lucky."

10

The journey back to Cusco was good fun. As we trundled into a Peruvian evening, the two train attendants (a young man and young woman) came around the carriage and sold us drinks. Soon the busy carriage was filled with laughter and frivolity.

Half an hour later, the attendants disappeared and some music came on: all pan pipes and haunting melodies. Then the young attendants reappeared. Instead of carrying drinks, they had donned alpaca clothing, and started wandering up and down the aisle modelling the wares on offer that could be purchased. With the music blaring, and the alcohol working its magic, the carriage soon took on a carnival atmosphere, with people clapping and cheering as each new article of clothing was shown. At one point, an elderly man got up to go to the toilet, and everyone clapped and cheered him. At first, he looked at little embarrassed, but then took it in good humour and even danced the last few steps.

The young woman was doing a fine job of modelling the clothes because she was selling lots of them. Even Angela wanted to buy some until I pointed out we didn't have enough Peruvian soles on us. But the woman across the aisle from us, a jovial Mexican-looking lady, spent a fortune. In the end, the attendants got her to model some clothes too, which she did with impressive swirls, hip sways and raucous laughter.

11

After the fun of the fashion show, we got chatting to our Mexican neighbours, except they turned out to be Texans. Three families, eleven people in total, four of them teenage kids, were sitting in a large group across the carriage.

"We moved to Texas twenty years ago," the smiling woman opposite me said. "All us adults were born in Mexico, but the kids were born in the States. They're Texan through and through."

"Is this your first time in Peru?" I asked.

The husband nodded. He had a drooping moustache and looked like a bandit. A friendly bandit though. "But we've been to South America before." Even though his accent was distinctly Mexican, there was a noticeable Texan twang hidden somewhere among the vowels.

"Yeah," said his wife. "We took our vacation in Santiago last year, and the year before that, we were in Bogota."

"So you can still speak Spanish?" I asked.

"Of course," laughed the woman. "Spanish is not something we can forget! We are all fluent in Spanish. Even the kids."

"So is Peruvian Spanish different from Mexican Spanish?"

"I'll tell you something we have noticed," she answered. "The Peruvians speak better Spanish than we do. More...I don't know...more...pure. And none of us has heard any cuss words from a Peruvian. In Mexico City, it is so different. Maybe Peruvians are more cultured than Mexicans."

As calm settled back over the carriage, the woman retrieved an iPad from her bag. She began flicking through photos she'd taken, occasionally pointing them out to her husband. "Hey," she said to Angela and me. "Have you guys tried cuy?"

We shook our heads.

"No, me neither. But I almost did." The woman explained that she had been seeking the strange delicacy out in Cusco. "We searched for a while and then came across a nice place, not far from the main square. We all sat down and when I told the waiter I wanted the cuy he spoke to another guy who led me behind the kitchen to an outside area. In the middle was a miniature house where all the guinea pigs lived. I'm not joking! It was like a dolls' house, with windows, doors and all sorts of crazy staircases. Some guinea pigs were running around, having fun; others were sleeping, and one was looking right at me from an upstairs window. The man asked me to pick one out so he could cook it! I told him, no way! I couldn't pick one out to die. They looked so cute. Anyway, I took a picture of the guinea pig house. Look."

Angela and I gawped at the photo. It was just as the woman had described: a large dolls' house filled with furry guinea pigs. There must have been thirty or forty of them in the various rooms, all looking like they enjoyed living there. There was no way I'd have been able to pick one out either.

An hour later, we arrived back in Cusco. As we said goodbye to our new friends, the man spoke up. "If you guys are ever in San Antonio, look us up. We'll show you the best places in town to eat."

We made a note of their email address and thanked them. We said goodbye and headed for a taxi.

12

The next day, our last in Cusco, Angela and I woke up with a headache again. The altitude sickness was still with us, though thankfully nowhere near as bad as it had been at the start. Both of us were sleeping longer and had regained much of our appetites; only the headaches doggedly remained.

"Do you think those Pisco Sours we had last night has made them worse?" asked Angela.

Pisco Sour is the national drink of Peru. It is a cocktail of lemon juice, egg white, syrup and something called Angostura bitters. It is so famous that Peruvians celebrate a public holiday in honour of the drink every February. In spite of the ingredients, the drink turned out to be delicious, and over the course of our evening meal, Angela and I had swilled a fair few glasses of the stuff.

"They probably didn't help."

We decided to visit an old Inca temple called Qorikancha, which was just around the corner from our hotel. I'd toyed with the idea of wearing my Panama hat again, but didn't want to stand out as a tourist buffoon in a city where pickpockets operated. I decided there and then to consign it to the bottom of my suitcase. I'd leave it for a decade and then try it on again.

Apparently, Qorikancha had been one of the most important temples in Cusco, covered from floor to ceiling in gold, and full to the brim with precious statues dedicated to the Sun God. When the Spanish found it, they had cooed with delight at riches 'beyond belief' and wasted no time in concocting a plan to get their hands on it. In the end, they captured an Inca leader, and then demanded a huge payment of gold to secure his safe return. When the Incas said they didn't have enough gold to pay the fee, the greedy Spaniards reminded them of the golden temple. Reluctantly, the Incas tore down the golden walls and statues and handed everything over to the Spanish, who melted the whole lot down. It took three days. In return, the Spanish executed the leader anyway, demolished the rest of the temple and then built a church on its grounds. Angela headed down some steps to the Qorikancha museum so we could see the tiny parts that remained.

"One hundred and thirty sol," said the woman behind the counter. "Each."

We quickly calculated this to be $90 for the pair of us! Maybe I'd misheard the lady, so I asked her to repeat the price.

"One hundred and thirty sol, each," she said more slowly.

I looked at Angela. She subtly shook her head. We turned tail and headed back up the stairs away from the most expensive museum in the world. For almost a hundred dollars, I'd have expected dancing girls, acrobats, magicians and a feast fit for an Inca King. We headed down Avenue de Sol towards a giant bronze statue.

13

The statue was huge. It was of an Inca emperor called Pachakuteq who had reigned from 1438 to 1472. Historians believe it was

Pachakuteq who had commissioned Machu Picchu, which had therefore made him the main man in Cusco.

Restaurants and hotels are named after him, and Peruvian coins depict his face, but the most visual presence of Pachakuteq is definitely his bronze statue at the end of Avenue El Sol. With his open-armed gesture (and a fearsome-looking spear in one hand), Pachakuteq looked quite friendly, but I knew from what I'd read that he wasn't quite so genial with people he didn't like. For instance, whenever he killed an enemy in battle, he enjoyed drinking from their skull, but only after he had pulled out the teeth and made flutes from their arms.

Pachakuteq was balanced on top of a huge round tower. As we got nearer, Angela noticed some people at the top and so we endeavoured to join them. Once inside, we were delighted to discover the entry fee was only two sol, and instead of cold stone steps leading upwards, we found a museum. A nice wooden staircase led us to rooms full of interactive displays and video screens.

"Look at this," I said to Angela. I was standing at a large display showing the Pachakuteq monument during an electrical storm. Angela joined me and I began to read the information below the picture. "It says that in 1992, when they were fitting the breast plate, three bolts of lightning hit the statue, even though there was no storm."

"Ooh! Spooky!" whispered Angela in mocking tones.

I shook my head. "I wouldn't say things like that. You might anger him. You might incur Pachakuteq's wrath."

"Ooh, I'm scared. Pachakuteq's wrath!"

We climbed the last remaining stairs to reach the summit of the tower. I looked upwards, barely able to reach the ankles of the seventeen-ton statue. The old Inca leader's monument was certainly an impressive piece of work and I wondered what he would think of modern-day Cusco, a place that probably wouldn't have existed in its present form without him.

"It's a good view," said Angela. We stood at the safety wall and looked down. Cusco was distinctly brown and low-rise, but the surrounding mountains offered a breathtaking vista. The air was crystal clear, one of those days where it was possible to see for miles, and even the large red billboard advertising something called *Maestro: especialista en precios bajos*, a specialist at low prices, couldn't spoil the view.

14

After some lunch, Angela and I were climbing a cobbled path up towards another Inca site. With the ever-steepening incline, the lack of oxygen in the air soon had us panting for precious breath. In England, the highest point is Scafell Pike, which measures a paltry 3208 ft. The Inca ruins we were scrambling up to were a ridiculous 12,142 feet above sea level, meaning we were getting about 40% less oxygen molecules into our lungs.

Ten minutes later, my breathing sounded like an accordion but without the melody. My pulse was rapid and I could feel my head throbbing. "This is it, Angela," I managed to gasp. "Death awaits. Don't forget the money in the safe...goodbye cruel world..."

As I slowed, looking for somewhere to collapse, an old woman carrying, of all things, a microwave oven, passed me from behind. She was grinning a toothless grin. "Buenos dias," she said as she disappeared around the mountain bend with ease and annoying dexterity.

Eventually, we made it to the entrance of the Saqsaywaman ruins (or Sexy Woman ruins as it's often called due to the similar pronunciation), where a man appeared. He was aged about thirty and had a clipboard.

"Hola," he said, smiling. "Americano?"

Angela shook her head. "English."

"Ah, Engleesh! Welcome to Saqsaywaman. You want to go in?"

I looked at the man but couldn't speak. I could hardly breathe. I was bent double, hands clasped to my knees, red forehead and misty eyes: the classic pose of the man about to die of a heart attack.

"How much?" Angela asked. She was proving to be far fitter than I was.

"Seventy sol each."

I raised myself upward. Seventy sol was about seventeen pounds; a bit excessive I thought, especially since it was just a pile of ruins.

"Yes, it is a lot, I know. But there is a cheaper way..."

"Oh?" I wheezed.

"Yes, you can hire a horse each. I will show you the ruins as we walk to my ranch. And then one of my guides will take you to the famous Sun Temple and Inca Tunnels."

"And how much would that be?" asked Angela.

"Forty-five sol each. What you say? My ranch is only eight minutes away."

"Oh, so you don't work here?" I asked.

"No. I work at the ranch."

I looked at Angela. I didn't really fancy riding on a horse, but I could tell Angela was excited by the prospect. Reluctantly, I nodded.

We nodded and began to follow him up the hill.

15

The journey to the horse ranch might have been eight minutes by helicopter, but not by the uphill trail the man was leading us along. I was wheezing once more and my only wish was for a comfortable coffin, preferably one with an oxygen mask inside, to take my final breath.

Angela looked at me in despair, informing me that I needed to do more exercise. I grumbled something in return and she turned her head.

"What?" she asked me.

"Nothing."

"Come on, what did you say?"

"Nothing." I forced my weary legs onward.

"Look," Angela said. "I'm nowhere near as tired as you, and that's because I do more exercise. You look like you're about to have a heart attack."

I grumbled something else. This time, Angela did not ask what the matter was.

We trudged onwards, scaling a mountain pass fit for a goat, and then, quite suddenly, we came to a plateau where an old woman was sitting with her llama. Behind her were the ruins of Saqsaywaman.

In its heyday, the walls of Saqsaywaman had made it an impressive Inca fortress. Towers lined its perimeter, protecting storage rooms and the other large buildings. When the Spanish came, they ripped everything down, and carted as many of the stone blocks away as they could. After they had finished building their own constructions in the centre of Cusco, only a few of the walls remained, the blocks too big and cumbersome for the Spanish to pilfer.

I stared at the ruins. To me, they resembled a set of dry stone walls common in rural England. They were better than that, of course, but nowhere near the league of Machu Picchu. I was glad we'd not paid 70 sol each to see them.

"Ranch not far," said the man. "We will soon be there."

16

Ten minutes later, I was sitting on my steed, feeling very uncomfortable. The last time I'd been on a horse was in Cairo, around the pyramids, but that had been on a flat plain. Here, it looked like we were going to climb a mountain pass without so much as a helmet or protective jodhpurs. As Angela mounted her beast, a boy aged about thirteen clicked his mouth and we set off. He followed from behind.

As we clambered up a steep trail, I grimly hung onto the reins and saddle, hoping I'd be able to keep my balance. I was fairly certain our travel insurance did not cover riding on the back of a horse up a mountain. I sneaked a quick glance behind me and saw that Angela was smiling.

I wasn't. I felt unsafe and unsteady. The horse also had an unappealing odour. "The reason why I'm struggling and you're not," I shouted back to my wife, "is because I'm from Roman stock. My ancestors were transported by chariot. Your ancestors were the Celtic hordes. Riding on a horse is natural to you."

Worryingly, just then, my horse decided to test this theory out. It veered away from the trail (despite me pulling on the reins) and began a climb up a rocky cliff face. Suddenly we were pointing at the sky and it was only by strangling the beast that I managed to cling on. After kicking its legs on the loose rubble, it righted itself but then stopped. My chest was thundering and I was breathing too quickly for my own liking, especially in the thin air. I looked back at Angela and she was shaking her head. That was it, I thought. I was getting off the damned thing. It had almost killed me and I'd only been on it for five minutes. Before I had a chance though, the boy in charge of the killer stallion made some clicking and whirring noise and my horse dutifully climbed back down from the ledge.

"We shouldn't be doing this," I said to Angela, a few minutes later.

"Oh we'll be fine," she said, holding onto her reins with what looked like practised ease. "Stop moaning."

"Did you see what just happened to me?" I said incredulously. "I could've died,"

Angela shook her head.

We reached the top of the hill and began a walk along a trail flanked by thick forest. The chirping of birds could be heard through it. I was thankful to be on a relatively flat piece of terrain for once. Just then, I heard the roar of a truck's engine. And then the sound of a car. We were coming to a road.

17

"Not again," I said to myself, feeling the horse increasing its pace. It had tried to kill me on the mountain and now it was going to finish the job on the road. I pulled the reins to slow it down, but it ignored my input. I kicked my legs on its bulbous fat body, but it carried on regardless. Behind me somewhere, the boy was clicking and whirring like mad, but it was to no avail. As for me, I had no time to consider the boy's antics because I could now see the strip of grey highway. It was crossing left to right, just ahead of the line of trees. A car raced past, and then a motorbike.

The boy was yelling now, but it was too late, we had reached the edge of the trees. As we sped past them, I closed my eyes and hung on as best I could. The impact would be immediate and deadly. Then we stopped. I opened my eyes and peered out. We were at the other side of the road. I let out a dreadful lungful of air as the nag lowered its head to munch on some weeds. While I regained my sanity, the boy ran across to join us. Incredibly, he was laughing. Angela was waiting at the other side of the highway, her horse under good control. She looked ashen, so I waved to tell her I was okay.

The boy took the reins and patted the side of the beast's head. "*Caballo travieso!*" he said, calling it a naughty horse.

"I want this horse arrested," I mumbled. "Or turned into glue." The boy smiled but couldn't understand me. I swallowed some more air, trying to get a grip on my breathing, and then attempted to climb off.

"No, no, estancia!" the boy said, telling me to stay. He took the reins and before I had chance to dismount, he was leading us back across the road. It was only now that I realised my thighs were burning and my hands were red raw. I had been gripping on for dear life.

18

"Are you all right?" Angela asked. She looked as shocked as I felt.

"I think so. My hands are a bit sore though."

"What happened? All I saw was you speeding off towards the road."

"God knows. It's this horse. It's possessed by Satan. When I came to the road, I just shut my eyes. I don't know how I made it across."

"You were lucky there were no cars going past. Thank God it's not a busy road."

"It's busy enough."

With the boy keeping my horse under firm control, we made our way to a pile of large rocks. The boy pointed at them, gesturing that we should climb off the horses and go and see them. "Inca tunnels!" he said, using English for the first time since we'd met him. "You...look! But no go in! Very dangerous."

Angela and I looked at the pile of boulders, now identified as Inca tunnels. They didn't look particularly impressive, but we felt obliged to see them up close.

We dismounted. Standing on terra firma, I looked at my horse. Now that the boy was holding it, it looked harmless and even friendly. But I could see the glint in its eyes. Given the chance, it would try again. I glared and it stared back. Then it lowered its head and began munching on some grass.

Up close, the tunnels were as we suspected – just a pile of boulders with a few cave-like gaps in them. They were about the right size for people to end up trapped. After a suitable time of staring at the rocks, we walked back to the boy and the horses. Mine flicked its forked tail and snorted fire from its nostrils. But after I'd climbed back on, it behaved itself, and twenty minutes later, we arrived at the Sun Temple.

19

The Sun Temple was another pile of rocks, this time with a plateau on the top. In fact, I wasn't really convinced it was a temple at all – there were no signs or notices indicating it was – and suspected it was simply a limestone hill. No matter, we climbed off our now well behaved horses and clambered to the top.

"Feeling better?" asked Angela as we negotiated our way across the rocky blocks. Without ropes and barriers, we would tumble down if we slipped.

"Just about."

We came to the edge, which offered a landscape of endless Peruvian plains. They ended only when they reached the mountains on the horizon. I turned around and noticed the young boy waving at us. "I think it's time to go back."

This time, the guide had a horse of his own, and took up the rear. I was at the front. After a few minutes, he clicked his voice and my horse began to trot. I steeled myself for another attempt on my life, my innards shaking like they were in a blender and my eyes wobbling uncontrollably in their sockets. From my shaky peripheral vision, I could see Angela was trotting behind me. As I clattered forwards, the idiot guide clicked again and we began a canter. The shift in speed was immediate. Roaring over a rock-strewn trail was now very frightening. I pulled the reins hoping it would stop the horse but it was useless; we hurtled onwards, passing another set of tourists – a trio of young women walking leisurely with their horses. We passed them in seconds and that was when I heard the scream.

Almost immediately, my horse stopped and I turned around to see Angela lying on the rocky terrain, one foot still in the stirrup, her back on the ground. The young guide was already dismounting his horse to help her. My wife was still, her face gazing up at the sky. Her horse was standing over her, already looking bored.

I climbed off my horse, rushing over to where Angela lay. Her eyes were open and blinking, and then she smiled. After the guide disentangled her foot, he helped her up. "You all right?" I asked.

Angela rubbed her arm and nodded. "I think so. But my shoulder is killing me, and my arm stings like mad." She twisted her arm and we both stared at the bloody scratch.

By this point, the group we had passed just moments before, approached, concerned about Angela's wellbeing, but our guide didn't seem bothered at all, despite being the cause of the accident. After informing the girls she was fine, they nodded and walked on. We followed on behind, ignoring the horses and the guide, who by now was hankering for a tip. A massive bruise was already forming on Angela's upper arm and the cut just below her elbow was bleeding quite badly.

She explained what had happened. "As soon as we started to canter, my foot came out of the stirrup and I started slipping. I knew I was going to fall. When I pulled the reins, nothing happened, except the saddle slipped. Then I did too."

I shook my head. "You were lucky. You could've landed on a rock and broken your neck, or worse."

"I know."

I spun around. "I know why it happened! It's the curse of Pachakuteq!"

"What?"

"You mocked his monument."

Angela smiled. "Yeah, maybe you're right."

By now, the guide had realised we were not going to give him a tip and so gathered his horses up. A minute later, he was walking off away from us. Angela and I made our way back down the hill towards the centre of Cusco. We vowed it would be the last time we rode on horses in South America.

That night was our last in the old Inca capital. The next day we had to be up early to catch a bus to Puno, the gateway to Lake Titicaca. And despite the horse incident, both of us had absolutely loved our time in Cusco. Angela was right, it was exciting to visit new places and experience new things. We were not jaded travellers; we were lucky travellers.

Top row: Plaza de Armas (main square of Cusco); View of Cusco from the Pachakuteq monument
Middle row: Delicious food items for sale in the central market; Indigenous women selling trinkets at a local market; Me as a brave Inca warrior
Bottom row: Machu Picchu; Pachakuteq monument; Street view of Cusco

Chapter 4. Lake Titicaca and the road to La Paz

Interesting fact: 60% of Lake Titicaca is in Peru, and 40% is in Bolivia.

Puno, the Peruvian town on the edge of Lake Titicaca, was an eleven-hour bus journey from Cusco. But this was no chicken bus filled with livestock, produce and locals; this was the Inca Express – a luxury coach equipped with air conditioning, TVs, a toilet and best of all, an attentive guide. As soon as we set off on our early morning departure, the man told us we would be making five scheduled stops: four to see some sights, one to have lunch. Then he served us some tea.

Angela and I settled back in our plush seats as the sun came up over the outskirts of Cusco. We soon hit the countryside, a landscape dominated by mountains, river plains and the occasional railway line. This was so much better than flying, I thought, to be out on the open road with the prospect of seeing Lake Titicaca at the end of it.

"How are your wounds?" I asked. The bruise on Angela's back was the worst one – a thick stain of blue, purple and red.

"Okay. My arm hurts a little, but my back only hurts if I twist it. It could've been much worse."

Our first stop was a small town with the almost incomprehensible name of Andahuaylillas, which was famous for its small church. Everyone on the bus duly trooped off and entered what the guide described as the Sistine Chapel of South America. From the outside, the church had looked unremarkable, but the inside was better, full of intricate paintings and golden statues, and though it was perhaps not quite in the same league as the Sistine Chapel, it was eye catching nonetheless. The guide led us around the interior, regularly stopping to explain about the various icons and artefacts. I quickly grew bored and when the opportunity presented itself (as the guide moved towards the rear of the church)

I slipped away, telling Angela I was going to find a toilet even though I didn't need to go.

Outside, I found an old woman wearing a traditional bowler hat. She was sitting on the church steps with her dog. When I proffered the dog some of the cake I'd nabbed from the hotel breakfast earlier in the morning, it immediately licked its chops in anticipation and then gently took it from my hand. The old lady smiled in thanks and so I gave her dog the rest of my cake. It was gone in seconds.

Ten minutes later, Angela joined me as she and the other Inca Express passengers erupted from the church entrance. She looked annoyed. "Why did you disappear like that? One minute you were there and the next you weren't."

"I was bored."

"So was I, but I didn't sneak away like you, pretending I needed the toilet."

I pointed at the dog. "I fed it my cake."

Angela loved dogs. Immediately, she smiled and bent down towards it. She stroked the animal's head and then fished around in her bag and found her cake. Like me, she offered it to the dog. It gobbled it down in two greedy mouthfuls. The woman nodded in appreciation.

We climbed aboard the coach for the next part of the journey.

2

Stop number two was some Inca ruins. The main section was a tall, thin wall, which a hawk had decided to make its nest on. We all had a good wander around the wall, but I was itching to get back on the road. Twenty minutes later, we were.

The third stop was lunch, which involved some live entertainment from a trio of musicians armed with panpipes, tiny guitars and percussion instruments between their knees. While they played their tunes, we all dined on alpaca steak and rice, the former tasty and lean. Afterwards, we all boarded the coach again for a gentle climb to 4318m (over 14,000 ft). The guide told us it was the highest point on the entire coach journey, and at the top, we would stop to take some photos.

A while later, our coach pulled over into a colourful tourist trap. Stalls selling alpaca scarves, hats, jumpers, rugs and much more besides were set out to entice us. Young girls wearing traditional costume waited with small llamas and alpacas, trying to catch people's attention as we trooped off.

It was chilly outside, but the views were stunning. Glacial snow had covered the peaks of the Andes, adding a great backdrop to the piles of alpaca clothing. Angela quickly succumbed to the temptation and bought herself a cheap jumper from one of the stalls. For one brief moment, we toyed with the idea of getting our photograph taken with the llama girls, but in the end, we shook our heads and boarded the coach. Ten minutes later, we lumbered onwards again, this time on a slight downward gradient.

3

"How cute are they?" Angela cooed on the next stop, as we stared at the group of vicunas, the domesticated ancestor to the alpaca and national animal of Peru. The five or six juveniles inside the enclosure looked like a cross between a Bambi deer and a furry camel. They had large dark brown eyes with massive eyelashes. If Disney wanted to make a film about them, people would adopt them as pets.

Everyone was straining to take photos of the vicunas or offering their hands for the inquisitive creatures to sniff. Inside the enclosure with them was a local man, littering the ground with corn.

"Come," said the guide. "There is a museum I want to show you."

Inwardly I groaned, but I followed everyone inside a small room. It was full of pots. I'd seen enough after just ten seconds and waited by the doorway. A small boy approached, proffering some tiny wooden carvings of what looked like alpacas. Angela joined me and looked at his wares, eventually picking two of them out.

"How much?" she asked.

The boy shrugged.

I handed him a five sol coin (80p), which he quickly pocketed and nodded. Twenty minutes later, we were all on the coach settling down for the final furlong into Puno. We'd been on the road for almost nine hours, but the time had passed quickly.

4

Suddenly, the bus came to a standstill. It looked like we had joined a traffic jam in the middle of nowhere. The driver switched the engine off and opened the doors. The guide stepped outside, presumably to find out the cause of the jam. On our left was a small river where bowler-hatted old women sat washing clothes. A few children ran past the bus, giggling, and then the guide reappeared. He picked up the microphone.

"Ladies and gentlemen. The reason we have stopped is because of a protest. Local teachers have blocked the road as a statement of their plight. I have just spoken to them."

Everyone strained to look ahead. In front of our bus were a few other vehicles and a crowd of people: the teachers, we presumed. Every now and again, we would catch sight of someone holding a placard.

"The government promised these teachers more money. They have now changed their minds. As it stands, they earn about 800 sol per month (£200), which is not enough, so I cannot blame them for striking. But don't worry, in thirty minutes they will allow us to pass."

The protest seemed a peaceful one, with an enterprising ice-cream seller pedalling up on his bike to set up shop. He soon had a roaring trade going, with protesters, observers and even some old women enjoying a cooling ice cream in the midst of a late-afternoon protest. In the end, the teachers removed the roadblock (after forty minutes) and allowed us passage.

5

We arrived on the outskirts of Puno as the sun was setting over the western horizon. For twenty minutes, we had been making our way down a winding mountain road until we had seen the town in the distance. In the fading light, Puno looked attractive, nestled on the side of some steep hills that led down to Lake Titicaca.

As we descended further, the grime crept into view, as did the slinking dogs that seemed to be patrolling most of the side streets. A trio of them were fighting along one darkened alleyway, while another couple humped by an overflowing bin. A smoke-belching dumper truck was slowing us down. It was going so slowly that a limping black dog had ample time to cross in front of it. We carried on through the town, hitting some thick traffic in the centre, and by the time we reached the bus station it was dark.

The bus station was a place of confusion. With the Inca Express delivering us at the stop, their job was done and we were on our own, trying to avoid the women attempting to flog us useless tat, and the men trying to tempt us into their taxis. We picked one man and dragged our suitcases to his car. He opened his car boot and shoved them in. We told him the name of the hotel, agreed upon a price, and were off. The hotel was not far, on the edge of the lake.

6

"Don't forget, we need to take our malaria tablets tonight," I shouted to Angela, who was busy in the bathroom having a shower.

"Okay," she shouted back.

I found the pack of tablets in my bag and removed two of them, one each, and put them on the bedside table. Ever since a hellish experience in Thailand when I'd opted for the cheapest brand of malaria tablet available, and then ended up with the most painful sunburn known to man, both of us now had the expensive, once-a-week Larium tablets.

I went into the bathroom to get a glass of water just as Angela was coming out. After filling my glass, I went to take my tablet but found it missing. I looked on the floor around the bedside table, and then under the lamp, but there was no sign of it.

"Have you seen my malaria tablet?" I asked.

"No."

"I left it on this table. With yours."

"With mine?"

"Yeah. One each. Like last time."

Angela rolled her eyes. "I've had both of them. I thought you'd left them there for me."

"One each," I said, sighing. I found the carton again. After removing another tablet from the blister pack, I washed it down with some water. "Good job we've got some spare ones."

During our horrendously expensive hotel meal (neither of us could be bothered trailing outside to find a local restaurant), Angela asked whether it was okay to take two Larium at once.

I shrugged. "I'm not sure."

"Well can you find out please, on the internet? We've got wi-fi, right?"

I nodded and typed *Larium* into Google, followed by *what happens if I take too much?* I quickly read what it said and looked up. "It doesn't sound good. It suggests we seek medical advice immediately."

Angela's face dropped. "You're joking, right?"

"No. It says even just one extra dose can cause problems. And, it also says you should never take them on an empty stomach."

"Really?"

"Yes. It says the overdose symptoms include vomiting, hair loss and peeling of the skin."

"Hair loss? Oh my God! My hair could fall out? And we're going to La Paz tomorrow. We don't have time to hang about in Puno to see a doctor! Why did I take two of them? I'm so stupid! Damn! Damn! Damn!"

I thought for a moment. "How long is it since you took them?"

Angela looked at her watch. "I don't know...maybe half an hour."

"And you feel okay?"

"Yeah, but that's not the point is it? They might have a delayed action"

"Look," I said, "it can't be that bad. This website says that people can take five of them in one go if they actually have malaria."

Angela looked unconvinced. "That's in an emergency where they might otherwise die." She stood up. "I'm going back to the room. I'm going to make myself sick. I just hope they haven't digested yet. Are you coming with me?"

I regarded my half-eaten meal.

"Fine," stated Angela, storming off.

I caught her up. "Stop worrying; you'll be fine. We'll sort something out. And besides, wigs are probably really cheap over here. I'll buy you a bowler hat."

Angela smiled thinly. Five minutes later, she was sitting over the toilet bowl with her fingers down her throat. After a few terrible retches, her meal came up and then so did a white frothy mixture that we hoped was the remnants of the tablets. She flushed the toilet and stood up.

"Job done," I said. "Drink lots of water and see how you are in the morning. In a day or two, take another tablet for the one you've just thrown up."

After another fitful night's sleep of tossing and turning, systematically gasping for oxygen or drinking water to moisten my dry throat, I awoke to find Angela already up and dressed.

"How do you feel?" I croaked.

"Fine. Hungry though. I need some breakfast. You sleep in, and I'll bring you back a croissant or something."

An hour later, we were both wandering around the hotel's grounds. Lake Titicaca looked magical, with an almost ethereal mist cloaking large sections of it. Later that morning, we would be taking a boat ride across it, something both of us were looking forward to doing.

As well as the lake, the grounds had a collection of cute, wild guinea pigs. The small mammals were enjoying the morning sun, some with their furry little heads turned up towards the sky, eyes closed and whiskers twitching. Watching a family of them for a while, I was glad I'd not eaten one in Cusco.

"Are you sure you feel okay?" I asked. "No stomach ache or anything?"

Angela shook her head. "I'm fine."

Soon it was time to leave Puno. Our day was going to be a long one, and would involve two guides: a Peruvian guide to take us to the border, and then a Bolivian guide to take us up to La Paz. The first guide was a friendly, fifty-something lady called Janeth. "It will take about two hours to reach the border," she told us, "but along the way you will see the beauty of the lake. Come, let's go to the car."

As we drove through the countryside of Peru, we passed more women in traditional costume – bowler hats, woollen shawls, long pleated skirts, long black braids and long socks. Angela asked Janeth about the hats.

"These women are Aymara: the indigenous people who have historically lived in the Andes of Peru, Bolivia and Chile. They are mountain people but the hats are interesting. Aymara women first started wearing them in the 1920s when a shipment arrived from Europe. The hats were not meant for the ladies but for railroad workers – to protect them from the sun – but the hats were too small for the men and so were given to the local women. They have remained ever since."

We passed a farmers' market filled with cows, sheep, pigs, llamas and alpacas. Two Aymara women were herding sheep while their men folk toiled in some fields close by. They seemed to be whacking piles of corn to remove the seeds. It was very medieval. None of the farms appeared to have any machinery at all.

"The Aymara people have nothing," said Janeth, "but they want for nothing too. Down there around the lake, they can fish for trout. Up here on the land, they can grow potatoes, and produce meat and milk from their animals. Some of the Aymara up in the mountains might breed alpacas, and on market day, they will swap produce with Aymara people who live in the lowlands. One might give an armful of alpaca wool for an armful of potatoes. Others will swap carrots and receive an armful of fish. No money is ever needed."

Eventually, we arrived at the Peru-Bolivia border. It was the usual chaotic scene of moneychangers, produce stalls, porters, border huts and people. But it was always exciting to be at a land border as opposed to arriving at an airport – things to see, people to watch, and the promise of a new country just metres away. After getting our passports stamped out of Peru, Janeth walked us past the parade of hawkers until we reached the Bolivian side.

"Okay," she said, "this is as far as I can go. Another guide will meet us here. I will call her now."

After a few minutes, a young, dark-haired woman approached and waved. We said goodbye to Janeth just as a coach load of tourists pulled up behind us.

"Perfect timing," said Janeth. "Have fun on the lake."

9

"Welcome to Bolivia," beamed Anna, our new guide. "Do you need to change any money?" I nodded and so Anna led us to a small money-changing booth where we swapped our remaining Peruvian sol into Bolivian bolivianos. As we walked towards the Bolivian border building to get our passports stamped, Anna explained a little about what we would be doing for the remainder of the day.

"First of all, we will have a walk around the little town of Copacabana. It's by the lake and is the *original* Copacabana. Then we will go on a boat ride and visit a couple of islands in the middle of Lake Titicaca. One of them, Isla del Sol, is where we will stop for lunch. After the boat tour, we will drive to La Paz where I'll drop you off at your hotel. How does that sound?"

We told her it sounded great, and I also complimented her on her excellent English. In fact, she sounded American to me.

"That's because I'm originally from New York. My father was American and my mother was Bolivian. When they divorced, I moved with my mom back to La Paz." Anna smiled. "As soon as I got here, I fell in love with the country. The clean air, the people, the jungles and the mountains. It made me proud to be half-Bolivian, something I never felt about New York."

Our entry into Bolivia was painless and didn't cost us a penny. American citizens were not so lucky, Anna told us. "They pay 135 bucks for a visa, which means most don't bother coming. It's because the US government makes Bolivians pay to enter the States, and so the Bolivian president decided to do the same. But it's so stupid. I mean, people from the States come to Bolivia to spend their money, to contribute to the economy, to have fun and then fly home. Most Bolivians who go to the States are looking for a new job and a new life. It's a totally different situation! But the Bolivian government are unable to understand this. They're cutting their own nose to spite their face."

Anna took us to a small white minivan and instructed us to climb aboard. We shoved our suitcases in the back and were soon driving the short distance to the border town of Copacabana.

"I hope," said Anna, "that you will see something exciting when we get there: maybe even something you've never seen before."

10

The town was packed because of something strange going on in the main square. Just outside the gates of a tall white basilica, lines of cars, minibuses and even trucks were waiting in untidy lines, all of them covered in flowers and flags. Crowds of people were in and among them.

"This is the Blessing of the Automobiles," explained Anna. "It happens every weekend in Copacabana. People bring their vehicles here from all around, to have them blessed by a priest, and then by a witchdoctor. Superstition is high in Bolivia and whenever someone buys a new car they will bring it here for the blessing."

Angela and I stared at the strange scene. Anna was right: neither of us had ever seen anything like it. White robed priests were splashing holy water over each vehicle in turn (and sometimes over people) and then another man – the witchdoctor, we presumed – lit firecrackers near the wheels. They crackled and danced like fireworks.

"After the car has been blessed," continued Anna, "the owner will spray champagne over it as an offering to Pachamama, the Earth Mother. She is important to the indigenous people of the Andes."

We left the car-blessing scene behind and walked through a colourful outdoor market. Piles of tomatoes, peppers and chillies were laid out on tables, with indigenous women in charge of selling them. Anna told us that in five days time, Bolivia would be celebrating its independence day, a festival of heavy drinking and hard partying. "And that is why Copacabana is busier than usual. The festivities will start today. People will start drinking soon. By this evening, everyone will be heading towards oblivion."

"I hope bus drivers don't drink," I joked. We had a two-hour ride to La Paz later that day.

"They do. And this is actually a big problem in this country. A lot of transportation workers get drunk and then drive passengers around. Not just during this festival, but all the time. It's a normal part of life in Bolivia."

"Really?" asked Angela. "Drivers could be drunk?"

"Yeah, really. But they hold a lot of power, these drivers. A while ago, the president stepped in to do something about them. It was after a spate of accidents involving drunk drivers. He announced on TV that it was against the law for any truck or bus driver to drink before they got behind the wheel." Anne shook her head. "The drivers couldn't believe it, so they got together and organised road blockades near La Paz. It brought the entire city to a standstill. Goods couldn't come in and nothing could get out. People had to walk to work, and no one could leave La Paz! But in the end, the blockade worked because the president changed his mind. So today, bus drivers can drink before they drive. It's crazy, I know, but that's how it works in Bolivia. The amount of power these drivers have is insane. They can hold the country for ransom whenever they want."

We walked to the edge of Lake Titicaca where a hydrofoil was waiting to take us to Isla del Sol, or Sun Island. The lake looked gorgeous, stretching to a horizon of jagged mountains. Copacabana's harbour was full of little pleasure boats, and it reminded me a little of a Mediterranean Sea port. In fact, the lake was so huge that it looked like a sea.

"Did you know that Bolivia doesn't have its own coastline anymore?" said Anna.

I nodded. I knew it was a landlocked country. But I wasn't aware that it had once had a coastline. I told Anna this.

"Yeah, it lost it to Chile over a hundred years ago."

11

In 1883, Chile, one of Bolivia's neighbours, decided it would like to own the phosphate-rich coastline belonging to Bolivia. It knew, of course, that Bolivia would not be happy about this, and would not simply hand it over, and so they waited for just the right moment to annex it.

The day they picked was a Bolivian festival, chosen because of the copious amounts of alcohol that most Bolivians would be drinking that day. True to fashion, the Bolivian border guards began boozing as soon as they awoke, quickly becoming merry and light-headed. After a few hours, they decided to have an afternoon nap so they could sleep off the excesses of the morning. This was when the Chilean troops advanced. The Bolivians were so comatose that all the Chileans had to do was simply move them to the side of the road. Then, once through the border, the Chilean soldiers marched to the coast and claimed it as their own. The Bolivian guards woke up and realised what had happened but couldn't do anything about it. Bolivia had lost its only section of coastline, mainly due to a drunken festival. Today, Chile still owns that coastline and tensions remain between both countries because of it.

12

Our fellow passengers to the Isla del Sol were a group of elderly Australian tourists. They had their own guide and were on a long trip around South America, visiting almost every country in the continent. After we'd all introduced ourselves, we settled down for the tour ahead.

Isla del Sol looked like a small rocky hill sprouting up from the tranquility of Lake Titicaca. It was cloaked in eucalyptus trees and its small harbour was nestled below a small hillside of agricultural terraces. Anna told us that the Island of the Sun had a small number of Inca ruins dedicated to the Sun God, which we wouldn't have time to visit. "But at least you will have a nice meal overlooking Lake Titicaca."

To get to the restaurant, we had to climb a set of steep steps (built by the Incas), which for once made me feel young and healthy. The pensioners were all gasping and wheezing after only a few steps, many of them standing against the railings, slack-jawed and on the edge of cardiac arrest. Angela and I sidestepped them like agile mountain goats and arrived at the top in no time at all, savouring the magnificent view below us.

"Wow," said Angela. "Just look at that." Both of us gazed at the expanse of delicious blue and the white-capped mountains of the Andes far in the distance. "It looks so peaceful and so...South American."

"How's your stomach?" I asked. Anna was talking to someone in the restaurant while we waited for the pensioners to catch us up.

"What about it?"

I reminded her about the malaria tablets.

"Oh yeah. It's fine, I think. I reckon we got away with it."

During lunch, Anna joined us, and I asked her about any annoying tour groups she'd had to deal with. She answered straight away. "As ashamed as I am to admit it, Americans are usually the worst. Recently I had a family from Atlanta, and I brought them to where we're sitting right now. They had two teenagers with them who did not appreciate where they were. Neither of them looked at the view, neither wanted to talk to me, and for the whole trip, both sat stony faced, staring into their BlackBerries, or else moaning about the lack of wi-fi signal."

A movement caught my eye. It was a man carrying a large sack on his back. Anne noticed him too. "That guy," she said, "lives on this island and it's his job to carry people's luggage from the boats up to a hotel on the top of the island. He'll have four suitcases in that sack, and he'll make the trip over and over each day. But the amazing thing is, he's 71 years old. Can you believe that?"

After lunch, it was time to visit the Fountain of Youth. Despite its promising name, the fountain turned out to be a trio of holes in a wall. Water gushed out from two of them (the third was dry). The holes weren't that big either, and the amount of water flowing out resembled a bath tap.

"When the conquistadores came," said Anna, "they believed this water could give them eternal life."

"Is it safe to drink?" asked Angela.

"Of course. Take some in your bottle."

Angela did and then took a sip. She nodded and passed it to me. It tasted like water.

"Okay then," said Anna. "Let's go to the boat. We'll visit Isla de la Luna, Island of the Moon now."

13

The even tinier harbour of the Island of the Moon had one jetty and a trio of women sitting on the floor with their trinkets laid out in front of them: belts made from alpaca wool, polished stones, wooden bracelets and a few necklaces. We stopped to look at them, and a couple of the Aussies bought a few things.

The Inca ruins were up on a high part of the island, which meant another power trip through the pensioners. It was amazing how our bodies had slowly adjusted to the high altitude of the Andes, and compared to our first few days in Cusco, we were more or less okay now.

At the top of the slope, Anna led us towards the Temple of the Virgins. The Australians were congregating around their own guide a short distance away. As we neared the ruins, I couldn't help but feel disappointed; the Temple of the Virgins was little more than a pile of rubble.

"There is not much left of the temple," admitted Anna, "but if you look over there, you will see a restored section." Angela and I stared at a line of mud brick terraced houses with Inca-style doorways. They looked okay, I conceded. I could almost imagine an Aymara virgin peering through the doorway, but only just.

"Before the Inca Empire," explained Anna, "there was the Aymara culture. The Aymara came to this island so they could train young girls to be wives for the elite. The girls learned how to be perfect wives for their future husbands. Every now and again, a rich man would come to the island to pick one of the girls out. Then they would sail back to the mainland to be married. But when the Incas took over, they changed the rules slightly. They imposed an age limit on the girls who could live here – they had to be between ten and fifteen – and they also made sure that the girls conformed to a certain set of physical features. Once a year, one of the girls was taken to the mountains for sacrifice."

"Sacrifice?" I asked.

"Yeah. For the girls, this was a great honour, and for their families too. In the months leading up to the sacrifice, the girls were fed the best food and were treated like royalty. To be chosen for sacrifice was the best thing that could happen to them."

During an Inca sacrifice, Anna explained, high priests would take a child to the top of a mountain. There, she would be given an intoxicating drink to make her amenable and less frightened. Finally, when the incantations were finished, the priest would whack the girl across the head and leave her to die on a burial mound. If the blow did not kill her, then the cold would.

In 1995, the preserved body of an Inca sacrifice victim was discovered. Because of the freezing temperatures of the Andes, the young girl's body was almost perfectly preserved. She was dressed in the finest clothes available at the time, and with her were a collection of statues, bowls and food items. Scientists estimated her age to be between 11 and 15, and worked out that she had died in the latter half of the 15th century. Her stomach contained a vegetable meal that she had eaten a few hours before she was killed, and when scientists looked into how the girl had died, they discovered a two-inch fracture in her skull, together with a cracked eye socket.

On the way back down to the lake, I asked Anna about the boat captain. I'd been wondering how he occupied himself while the rest of us trailed around the sights. Anna laughed. "Don't worry about him. He is okay. He has a girlfriend on this island. He'll have kept himself busy, if you know what I mean."

"So he's not married?" asked Angela.

"Oh yes, he's married, but this sort of arrangement is not so strange for men in Bolivia. The only rule, I think, is not to have an affair with your neighbour's wife. But for women, it is a different matter. Let me tell you something: if a woman did the same thing as the boat driver, she would be shunned. Her family would cut off her long hair or braids, which, for an Aymara woman, is the worst thing that can happen. It is so shameful that she would have to leave her home and live elsewhere."

Our short tour of Lake Titicaca had ended. Anna took us to the bus that would take us on the next stage of our journey. We waved goodbye to the lake, to Copacabana, and looked onward towards La Paz.

Top row: A traditional boatman on Lake Titicaca; Cute guinea pig – tasty! The highest point we got to en route from Cusco to Puno

Middle row: Adorable vicuna, relative of the alpaca; Angela and me on Isla de la Luna

Bottom row: Blessing of the Automobiles; the lakeside at Copacabana

Chapter 5. La Paz and the Llama Foetuses

Interesting fact: The world's most dangerous road is in Bolivia, the so-called Road of Death. We didn't go on it.

The bus journey to La Paz from Lake Titicaca took us through yet more breathtaking scenery. A golden landscape of remote villages, isolated dwellings and river plains, all under the majesty of the Andes, made the trip one to savour.

The minivan we were in wasn't quite as delightful. Numerous warning lights flashed up on the dashboard – messages such as CHECK TYRE PRESSURE, OIL CHANGE REQUIRED and the worrying BRAKES NEED TESTING. But at least the driver was sober. Just over an hour later, we approached the city of El Alto.

At one time, El Alto had been a suburb of La Paz, but because of its size, in 1985, it became a city in its own right. It had a population of over a million, the vast majority of whom were Aymara people. As we passed through it, El Alto looked down-at-heel, a dirty frontier town, unkempt and unloved. Most of the buildings looked broken and unfinished, and the lack of street lighting added to the sinister feel, especially as night fell across Bolivia.

"El Alto is growing at an alarming rate," explained Anna. "It is the fastest growing city in South America. But this has major implications for the government. The crime rate is astronomical, with gang fights and murders all the time. But there are also other problems here. About half of the population of El Alto have no running water or electricity."

The main road through El Alto was a cacophony of beeping and crowds. Anna pointed out something. "Have you noticed the scarecrow-type figures hanging from some telegraph poles?"

We had. Most of the dummies had been hanging by nooses, but a few were attached with lengths of rope. Some were dressed in Tshirts and trousers, sometimes with coats and hats on. They resembled Guy Fawkes effigies. All looked ominous.

"They're there to warn people that *Community Justice* rules the area. This is a form of law brought down from the mountains, and basically means lynch mobs operate."

"Lynch mobs?" Angela asked.

"Yeah. But Community Justice only affects the indigenous population."

"And they allow that sort of behaviour here?" I asked.

"I know it seems strange, but in the mountains, where there are no police or law enforcement officers, people have become used to dealing with crime themselves. And since most of the people living in El Alto are originally from the mountains, it's natural for them to have Community Justice here. Whether that's a good thing is another question."

We passed a white painted message on a wall. Anna told us it said that if a thief was caught in the neighbourhood, they would be burned alive."

"My God," said Angela.

"I know. Sometimes the police will come, but if they do, they are usually outnumbered by the mobs. Besides, the people of El Alto don't trust the police much anyway. Whenever they've handed thieves over to them in the past, the police have taken whatever they've stolen and then released them. Community Justice solves this problem."

I looked at Angela. She looked as shocked as I did. I couldn't quite get over the fact that the government of Bolivia allowed such a thing to happen. "So let me get this straight," I said to Anna. "Community Justice is people sorting out their own punishment for a crime committed here?"

"Yes."

"And there is no trial or investigation. It's just a lynch mob setting someone on fire?"

"Basically, yes. If a person steals something, and is caught, they will be killed. Simple as that. This is Community Justice. If a person rapes someone, they will be killed. Community Justice. And the Bolivian constitution allows this. A person will not go to court if they can prove they have killed someone as a punishment. But the big problem with Community Justice is that sometimes the vigilantes get the wrong man. Maybe one, two or three people are killed before the right man is caught. And what will they say to the innocent man's family? Oh, hey, I'm really sorry about murdering your son; here's a bag of potatoes."

We sat in silence as we drove through the mean streets of El Alto. Despite the shadows, things looked calm. The people crossing the road looked friendly enough, and the storefronts were busy with women trying to buy the last of the day's fruit and vegetables. There were no lynch mobs in operation, at least as far as we could tell.

"Not long ago," said Anna, "a police officer was lynched here. He was enjoying a night out, off duty of course, and decided to leave the nightclub he was in. For some reason he got lost and ended up trying to get inside a school building, perhaps to sleep. The school caretaker woke up, thought he was a thief, and gathered some neighbours. They killed him."

We passed the blurred boundary between El Alto and La Paz and began a descent into the canyon. La Paz was contained wholly within the bowl, and we could see the lights twinkling on all sides. As we drove even lower, the difference between El Alto and La Paz could be seen easily. For a start, the buildings looked in better shape, with even a fair smattering of modern-looking skyscrapers, and there was more street lighting. The city centre was packed to high heaven with cars, vans, buses and people. The last time I'd seen such a mass of humanity had been in Bangladesh.

"Welcome to La Paz," said Anna as we drove bumper to bumper through a main street. "Tomorrow, make sure you visit the

Witches' Market and Plaza Murillo. But don't walk too quickly; the air is still very thin in the mountains."

We pulled up outside our hotel said goodbye to Anna. She had been a fantastic guide from start to finish.

2

The next day, we awoke to glorious sunshine. The weather on our South American trip had been perfect throughout, despite it being winter. We left the hotel and headed out to see the sights of La Paz.

"It's not a very pretty city, is it?" said Angela as we walked up the main street, passing men selling Bolivian flags, and people standing around waiting for minibuses. Street stalls sold the usual soft drinks, cigarettes, newspapers and chocolate bars, and in the clogged-up roads, blue Dodge buses chugged along with a never-ending cavalcade of white minivans.

Despite La Paz translating to *The Peace*, it was anything but. Beeping horns, clattering wheels, raucous chattering and the occasional barking dog made it a noisy, busy city. But Angela was right about La Paz not being very pretty. Apart from a collection of modern-looking skyscrapers in the city centre, many of the buildings looked run down and grubby.

In the hills, it was a different matter. Up there, La Paz looked great. Packed among the slopes were multitudes of simple orange and brown brick buildings. They filled the entire hill slopes. The higher they were, the poorer the people who lived in them were. But with some snow-capped mountains in the distance, and a morning sun casting a pleasing glow over them all, I could see why some thought La Paz beautiful, at least from certain angles.

"Look at those two." Angela was staring at a busy road running parallel to ours. Two people were dressed up in zebra costumes and were waving their arms about and running on the spot. One was carrying a sign saying: PARE, which meant stop, the other had two chequered flags. As we watched in amusement, one of them entered the road and, when the traffic had stopped, danced about while people crossed over.

We came to Plaza San Francisco, a rather grand name for a nondescript square. The only building of note was the San Francisco Church, which looked like it also doubled up as a museum. Plenty of people were milling about, most waiting for the minibuses to pull in. Women in bowler hats stood in the middle trying to sell trinkets, but we walked past them, turning uphill towards the Witches' Market.

3

The Witches' Market is perhaps the most famous tourist attraction in La Paz, despite not being for tourists. Angela and I were not sure what we were looking for, though, and so when we reached where we thought the market was supposed to be, we were disappointed to find only a few stalls, similar to all the other ones we'd already passed.

Consulting the map, we retraced our steps. "What is the Witches' Market supposed to look like?" Angela asked.

I shook my head. "No idea."

An Aymara woman walked by. Instead of a bowler hat, she was sporting a brown woolly number, and she appeared to be carrying half a shop on her back. The large bundle was packed to the brim with similar hats.

"It's got to be somewhere around here," I announced, looking back along the street we had just walked along. "Maybe back down there."

Strings of telegraph wires hung over the street, gathering in deep, dark coils around the top of the poles. A man with a set of scarves dangling over his arm approached us, proffering his wares. We smiled but shook our heads and set off walking again, quickly arriving at an intersection with a few random stalls covered with blue tarpaulin. Underneath the plastic sat women in colourful shawls. And then we saw the set of dangling llama foetuses; they looked gruesome. We had found the Witches' Market.

Some of the dried foetuses were small and brown, little more than skin and bones. But some were large and looked almost fully formed, with a cloaking of white fur. One particular harrowing foetus had its eyes open, eyes that had never seen outside of its mother's womb. The woman in charge of the stall stared at us with suspicion. I asked if we could take a photo of her stall, but she shook her head and scowled.

We walked past the stall, now seeing quite a few other similar ones. Most were congregated on the corner of the street, but others were actual shops. As well as llama foetuses, the stalls sold herbs, feathers, dried frogs and insects. I also knew that there would be less appealing things inside some of the shops. In dark recesses, I'd read, puma skins and tarantulas could be bought, all of them kept well away from the prying eyes of inquisitive tourists.

The main customers of the Witches' Market were the indigenous people of La Paz. They bought the items so they could make offerings to Pachamama, the Earth Mother. They would take their purchased foetuses to a local witch doctor (where the name Witches' Market comes from) who would then make the offering on their behalf. Whenever anyone bought or made a new house, for instance, a llama foetus was put in the foundations for good luck.

"It's usually poorer people who buy these foetuses," I told Angela, as we stared at a particularly horrible set of dangling foetuses. Their furry bodies and unformed limbs made for upsetting viewing. "Rich people usually sacrifice live llamas to Pachamama."

The beginning of August was a particularly busy time for the Witches' Market in La Paz because it tied in with midsummer. People bought offerings and took them to the highest point in the city. Witch doctors would be on hand to offer their services, which usually amounted to setting the foetuses alight (often with other choice items, such as cigarettes, alcohol and money), and then chanting incantations in the name of the person who had provided the offerings. That done, the witch doctor buried the smouldering pile, meaning the person could get on with their lives, safe in the knowledge that Pachamama would be watching over them.

"It's horrible," said Angela as we walked past a few more stalls. "And I know it's a tradition, but look at those poor llamas. Not even born. I think we should leave."

4

We headed across the other side of the city to a place called Plaza Pedro D Murillo. It was the best looking part of La Paz by far, surrounded on all sides by grand, Spanish-built colonial buildings. The President's Palace (complete with red-uniformed guards) and La Paz Cathedral looked the best, all domes, columns, flags and statues, but the centre of the square caught our eye most; it was a frenzy of pigeon feeding, with birds sitting on people's arms or crowding their feet. One small girl was covered in pigeons, giggling with delight, even though to us the scene looked slightly disturbing.

We decided it was time to find a cafe and the one we found was just off the square. While Angela busied herself at the counter, I began flicking through an English language newspaper I'd picked up in the hotel. As well as the usual stories of email hacking and footballers wanting unreasonable wage increases, there was a story about a local politician being stalked by a woman. The story wasn't particularly interesting, but when Angela returned, she noticed the headline.

"You had a stalker once, didn't you?"

I looked up and smiled. She was right. When I'd been at university, I'd had my very own stalker, something I was quite proud of.

I'd been enjoying a night out with my friends when an attractive girl approached me. She told me her name was Debbie and that she was a student nurse. I'd never seen her before, but being a young man, free and easy (I'd just split with my girlfriend the weekend previously), we chatted and then danced, and at the end of the night we had gone back to her apartment.

It didn't take long for me to notice the small framed photo of myself on Debbie's bedside table. It was almost hidden behind a lamp, but my eye had caught it nonetheless. I looked again, hoping I was mistaken, but I was not. It was definitely me: my image staring back at me from a room I'd never been in before. Debbie was unaware that I'd noticed it, chatting away about this and that, but I don't remember a word of what she said. All I can recall was feeling worried and confused. After thanking Debbie for the glass of wine, I made my excuses and left.

How had she got the photo, I wondered as I rushed home? And why had she framed it? Worse still, why had she left it on her bedside table? And what else did she have that belonged to me? I was thankful I did not own any rabbits. My mind spun with the possibilities of it all. When I told my friends, they laughed and then one of them told me I had a stalker, and that Debbie sounded like a nutcase.

A few weeks later, after avoiding the nightclub where I'd met Debbie, and looking over my shoulder a lot, one of my friends told me something interesting. He'd been in a bar the previous evening and had met a girl who had turned out to be one of Debbie's friends.

The girl explained a few things about Debbie's fixation with me. It had all started when Debbie had seen me in a nightclub a few months previously. At that time, I'd been with my then girlfriend and so Debbie had kept her distance. But one night, she decided to follow me home to find out where I lived. With one of her friends, Debbie trailed me (from a discreet distance) to my student accommodation: a large house I shared with six of my friends. Once they had discovered my address, the girls returned to their own apartments where Debbie manufactured a reason to visit.

A few days later, after waiting for me to leave, Debbie and the same pal knocked on the door, explaining that they were interested in looking around the house, as it might suffice for them the following academic year when we moved out. This was a reasonable request, and one we were quite used to, and so they were shown around the various rooms, including the cellar. In the cellar was a dartboard with seven passport photos pinned onto it, one for each student who lived in the house.

The photos had been on the dartboard for a silly reason. When we'd first moved in, one of us had come up with a scheme. The person whose photo ended up with the most holes by the end of the month had to buy everyone else a drink. It was a stupid idea and we'd all quickly tired of the game, leaving the photos to languish at the bottom of the basement stairs. And that was where Debbie had stolen my photo.

"You've made that up," said Angela, after I'd retold the tale, even though she'd heard it before. "As if *you* had a stalker!"

I shrugged. "It's true. All of it. How could I make up a story like that? And besides, I was a love god back then. I was like John Travolta in Grease."

Angela shook her head and smiled. "Did you ever see Debbie again?"

"Funnily enough, yes. About six months later, we were all out in a nightclub – a different one from where I'd first met her – and I saw her by the bar. She didn't see me and so I just ran out. That was the last time I saw her. She's probably a nurse now, and her home is a shrine to me. Pictures of me, effigies that she's made from clay, love letters, the lot. God help me if I ever end up in a hospital where she works."

Angela laughed. "She wouldn't want to stalk you now, that's for sure."

I raised my eyebrows. "Thanks."

"No problem."

Angel and I began randomly wandering up and down steep streets, passing elegant churches, plenty of museums, cracked pavements and tiny bars that offered karaoke. At one point, we heard the pounding of drums, so stood and watched as a troupe of drummers marched along a street parallel to ours. Soon they disappeared from sight, with only the pounding of their drums audible as it reverberated around the buildings.

We carried on walking up a horrendously steep street towards a large outdoor market. Ladies sat waiting for customers, with fish, fruit, and masses of potatoes for sale around their feet. Standing over one stall was a man in dreadlocks, and as we passed him, we caught the unmistakable aroma of marijuana.

There just wasn't that much to do in La Paz, Angela and I realised. From what we could gather, we had seen most of the major sights, and unless we wanted to induce a heart attack by climbing further upwards, we were tied to the lower levels. We headed back down to the main street.

"It's an interesting place," said Angela, "but not a beautiful one. I'm glad we're not here for much longer. Tomorrow we're going to Santa Cruz, right?"

I nodded. The next day we were flying to the Bolivian city of Santa Cruz, a place neither of us had heard of until just before the start of our South American jaunt. Originally, our plan was to fly from La Paz to Asuncion, the Paraguayan capital, but that was before the airline operating that route had gone bust, leaving us in the lurch. After looking at alternative means of transport between the two cities, I quickly found out there was a coach to Asuncion, which someone on the internet described as 'three days of hell' in an 'old dilapidated bus'. Instead, I found a cheap flight with an overnight connection in a place called Santa Cruz. We would stay there for one night and then fly to Asuncion the day after.

"And we finally leave the Andes," I said. "We'll be able to breathe properly."

"Yeah, just as we're getting used to the thin air."

The headaches had gone, we were sleeping well and our appetites were back to normal. And we'd done it without pills, coco leaves or witch doctors.

6

The next morning, we made our way to the airport. The flight was uneventful except for some kind of electronics failure in the cabin. It forced the cabin crew to make all their announcements by handheld loudspeaker. No matter, the flight landed an hour later in tropical Bolivia.

We were back in a land of palm trees and green jungle, but Santa Cruz itself looked uninspiring: a mess of graffiti and generic buildings. It was Bolivia's largest city and its economic centre. Hardly anyone was dressed in traditional clothes. It seemed we had left the indigenous people behind in La Paz.

The taxi dropped us off at our hotel, but instead of venturing out to see what the city had to offer, we simply lazed by the pool, savouring the oxygen-rich atmosphere after spending so long in the mountains.

Our time in Bolivia was almost at an end. Next destination: Paraguay.

Top row: Look how hilly La Paz is; Llama foetuses for sale in the Witches' Market
Middle row: Indigenous women of La Paz; A more modern side of La Paz; Ceremonial guards in Plaza Murillo
Bottom row: La Paz street scene; Plaza San Francisco

Chapter 6. Down and Out in Asuncion

Interesting fact: Apparently, duelling is legal in Paraguay as long as both people are blood donors.

Most people who visit South America miss Paraguay out. As Angela and I sat in the back of a taxi, bouncing along the uneven road towards the centre of Asuncion, we quickly realised why. Broken down buildings, cracked pavements, groups of teenagers swilling cans of lager in a city square, Paraguay's capital was a dirty, down-at-heel place that seemed to know that tourists were not going to come and had therefore given up any semblance of making the place look nice.

"Do you know what it reminds me of?" said Angela half an hour later. We were walking along a street near our hotel. Evening was fast approaching, and graffiti was everywhere. "A rough council estate in Northern England. I can't believe this is the capital of Paraguay!"

I had to agree. After visiting cities across more than ninety countries, Asuncion had to be close to the bottom. In fact, I was struggling to think of a less appealing place I'd been to. We turned off one street and onto another. Dirty buildings were all along it, as was the occasional policeman carrying a hefty automatic weapon. Suddenly, a loud hollering caught our attention. A crowd of men were huddled around a small outdoor TV showing a football match. From somewhere else a dog barked, its yaps reverberating around the bleak buildings of downtown Asuncion. Yes, I thought, we've finally hit rock bottom.

2

So why did we include Asuncion in our South America trip? Good question. There was a simple answer though: no one ever went there. People went to Rio, people went to Machu Picchu, and people went to Santiago in Chile. Plenty of travellers also visited

Argentina and Uruguay, and plenty more went to countries like Ecuador, Colombia and Venezuela. But no one ever went to Paraguay, so that was why I'd included it in our itinerary. A silly reason, really.

"I knew we shouldn't have come here," said Angela. We were traipsing back towards the hotel, hoping to spot a decent restaurant on the way. "I didn't even want to come."

"I know. But at least we're only here for one night."

We couldn't find a restaurant that was open. Indeed, the only places that seemed to be doing any business at all were a few bars and one small shop.

"Jesus," whispered Angela as we browsed the threadbare shelves of the shop. A few tins of this, a few packets of that: it was as if we were in Eastern Europe during the communist days. Angela had been hoping to buy a bar of chocolate, but the only thing on offer was a packet of chocolate-covered wafers. "Get me out of this God-forsaken place," she said, a stunned expression on her face.

Back at the hotel, after eating an overpriced meal in the in-house restaurant, we retired to our room. On the ceiling, next to the strip light, was a hook. When I pointed it out to Angela she said, "That's for the noose when you've had enough of Asuncion."

3

Paraguay had been through a rough time, though. Despite being the first South American country to declare independence from Spain, it quickly found itself in the hands of a mad dictator called Jose Gaspar Rodriguez de Francia.

Francia was the first in a long line of Paraguayan crackpots. As soon as he came to power, he began cracking the whip with gusto, not concerned in the slightest that people might consider him a despot. In fact, his official title was *Supreme and Perpetual Dictator of Paraguay*, so it seemed Francia was not bothered at all.

He quickly banned opposition parties and then created his own secret police. He also established his very own prison called the Chamber of Truth. Inside its dank walls, anyone the president didn't like was tortured until they confessed the truth: that they were traitors to the country. For his own entertainment, Francia had a large window installed in his palace. He then made it mandatory for all executions (and there were many) to take place outside it. It was a nice distraction while he sipped on his afternoon tea.

Politics wasn't his only area of madness; Francia particularly distrusted marriage, to the point where anyone who wanted to be betrothed had to pay a huge tax to the government, and then had to have Francia conduct the wedding himself. These measures usually were enough to put most people off.

Francia didn't like the idea of marriage because he liked the freedom to have affairs with as many different women as he could. Indeed, he ended up fathering seven illegitimate children in the process, and when one grew up to be a prostitute, Francia declared it a legitimate profession.

During his 26 years of absolute power, Francia became the victim of so many assassination attempts that he created a bewildering array of ruses to combat attempts on his life. He outlawed bushes along any street he wished to walk upon, thereby rendering hiding places for assassins obsolete. He took to sleeping with a gun under his pillow, and because he slept in a different bed every night, this meant a lot of guns. Nobody was allowed within six paces of the dictator, and if any local person happened to encounter him on the streets of Asuncion, they had to immediately throw themselves to the pavement or else risk being shot. Also, in an unprecedented act of paranoia, he ordered his own mother killed, fearing that she wanted to usurp his presidency.

So with a despot like that in charge, it wasn't surprising that Paraguay ended up being a little off kilter.

The next morning, Sunday, even the weather got in on the act of making Asuncion look grim. It was overcast and grey, adding a further element of gloom to the city. We'd read that Asuncion on Sunday would be like a ghost town, but as we wandered around, we decided it was more like a scene from an apocalyptic horror film. Shambling wrecks, sometimes by themselves, but mostly in pairs, were wandering around, often grinning, always scary. As we walked down one deserted street, we heard a god-awful clattering behind us; we turned to see a man pushing a supermarket trolley down the middle of the road. In the trolley were a human skull and a bag of dead pigeons (actually, there was nothing inside it at all). When he passed us, the man turned to stare, an open expression on his face. We turned up another street and passed a comatose tramp curled up in a doorway. His bare feet were cracked and blackened. All Asuncion needed was a black crow sitting on a lamppost and the scene would be complete.

"I thought it might look better this morning," I commented. "But if anything, it's worse."

"You don't say," replied Angela, sidestepping some dog mess lying in the middle of the pavement.

Many of the buildings around us were dirty and in need of repair, some even looking like they had been gutted after some terrible fire. Decrepit buses rumbled up and down the uneven streets and dogs barked at us from high fences. Asuncion was the city of the damned.

In Plaza de los Heroes, we thought we might find a semblance of beauty but instead we found a dirty green park with a statue in the middle. Another vagabond was asleep on a nearby bench. The statue's base was covered in graffiti and someone had even managed to place a plastic bottle in one of the statue's hands. The place looked unloved and forgotten, much like the rest of Asuncion. What made it worse was that the plaza was actually a memorial to all Paraguayans who had died in the Paraguayan War of 1864.

In that year, the country had battled not one of its neighbours, but three. Brazil, Argentina and Uruguay took to arms against their landlocked neighbour over a territory dispute. With such a huge force against them, the Paraguayans didn't stand much of a chance, and were soon losing on every front. Indeed, by the latter stages of the war, Paraguay was sending its soldiers into battle without weapons. They were expected to take them from the enemy. In the end, the triple alliance utterly defeated Paraguay, devastating the country's economy and decimating its population. More than 60% of Paraguay's population died in the war, which meant that in some parts of the country, the ratio of women to men was 20 to 1.

Angela and I stared at the monument. "You'd think," I said, "that the locals would look after it a bit more. They don't seem to have any respect for their own city." We left the park by its northern entrance and headed towards the river.

5

A car passed us and its driver threw his rubbish out of the window. A few metres more and he tossed some more out. Angela shook her head. "Well that just about sums up this place. No wonder it's so run down."

Down near the river, Asuncion took a turn for the worse. Rough tracks, shanty dwellings and people hanging around on walls made us quicken our pace. When I tried to take a photo, a man shouted at me, waving me off. The presence of the brown-uniformed police didn't help much either. The Paraguayan police were renowned for their bribe taking and corruption. I doubted they would be much help if we were mugged. Mind you, there were plenty of pharmacies to buy some bandages and bruise cream. They seemed the most popular type of trading establishment in the city. That said, I'd read that Asuncion was actually one of the safer South

American cities, with violent crime rare. But if that was true, why were most of the militia decked out in what looked like riot gear?

The river looked okay though, and on the other side was Argentina. I speculated whether people ever swam across to their richer neighbour, hoping for a better life. Perhaps to counter this, a small naval vessel was moored by the shore on the Paraguayan side, but it looked like it hadn't been out in a while.

We wandered away from the river towards a nearby cathedral, which turned out to be nice enough, as was the Cabildo, a large pink building that had once housed the government, but was now a museum. Just next to it was an abandoned bus. Scores of small children were messing about inside, laughing and joking and having a merry old time. Some were sitting on the driver's seat, others hanging out of the window, and we left them to it, soon arriving at possibly the best-looking building in the whole of Asuncion – the President's Palace.

The grand white building, shaped like a flat letter 'U', overlooked the river. In front of it was a parade of Paraguayan flags together with a manicured garden. Compared to everywhere else in the city, this was paradise. The guard on duty at the front even allowed us to take a few photos. When Paraguay had been under the control of its dictators, people lingering for too long in front of the palace would have earned a bullet in the head.

We wandered back towards the hotel, thinking of what to do next. Suddenly, a beggar approached, a young girl aged about ten. She was dressed in a scruffy T-shirt and shorts. Her feet were bare.

"Guarani, guarani," she wailed. "Por favor, Senor!" Guarani was the local currency, and since she appeared to be the only beggar in the vicinity, I passed her a couple of coins. She accepted them and smiled sweetly.

Angela and I walked away, sidestepping the cracks in the pavement and avoiding the stares of men sitting around on plastic chairs.

Our hotel room had a tray filled with things such as coffee sachets, mints, mini bottles of whisky and headache pills in single packs. Each item had a price sticker attached, and when I picked up one of the pills, I found out its cost was a thousand guarani (15p). Headache tablets, sold singularly, were something I'd never seen for sale in any hotel before.

"The view is nice," said Angela, stepping out onto the small balcony. I joined her, gazing out at the dismal sight before us. Asuncion really was a dump. Apart from the few nice areas we'd visited earlier, the city was nothing more than a rotting concrete jungle. A particularly bad offender was a 15-storey block that looked like it belonged in a Third World country. The top half was black with grime, and one side of it was taken up by a faded Coca-Cola advertisement. I'd seen similar-looking buildings when I'd been in the Bangladeshi capital, Dhaka. Broken-down buildings and ugly mobile phone masts made up the rest of Asuncion's horizon. The only redeeming features were the palm trees and snippets of the River Paraguay in the distance.

"Let's find somewhere to eat," I said.

The place we found was busy. A smiling man led us to a table and told us it was buffet serving only. "Juicy steak!" he said. "Very cheap!"

He was right. The steaks were very juicy and extremely cheap. And unlike the streets outside, the place was full of people in good cheer. The sound of raucous laughter could be heard at the table next to ours – an extended family of kids, adults and oldies, all enjoying a good meal together. It was a similar deal across most other tables. It seemed we had found the happy place in Asuncion.

"This steak is delicious," commented Angela. I nodded, chewing my own. I'd heard that the steak in South America would be something to die for, but I never expected to find it in Paraguay. "Argentina has a lot to live up to after this."

After lunch, we looked in the guidebook again. It appeared we'd seen most, if not all, of the sights Asuncion had to offer. Except for one: an abandoned railway carriage.

"An abandoned railway carriage?" scoffed Angela. "Why would I want to see that?"

I smiled and shrugged. "Because there's nothing else to see. We've got ages before we have to go to the airport."

The Paraguayan railway system was one of the first in South America. It was meant to signify great change for the country, allowing trade and money to creep in, but following the disastrous Paraguayan War, things went downhill and the railways fell into neglect.

Today, the country has hardly any trains to speak of, and most of the railway lines have been covered up by vegetation. A short distance from the restaurant, we found the remnants of Asuncion's railway station. In its heyday, it had probably been a grand building, full of life, with the prospect of economic salvation to boot.

"Is that it?" said Angela, shaking her head. "We've trailed all this way to see that?"

It did look pretty bleak, I had to admit. The station (supposedly a museum now) looked like it was falling apart, with metal girders and loose wires all over the place. The wooden carriage inside an old platform looked sad and abandoned too, sitting stationary on rusted tracks.

"Let's head back," I said. "I think we've seen enough." We set off the way we had come, along the way feeding a stray cat some scraps of meat we'd taken from our meal earlier. It looked like it hadn't eaten in days.

Back in our room, both of us were glad our short time in Paraguay was almost at an end. We tried to think of anywhere else we'd been that was as bad as Asuncion, but couldn't.

After we'd packed our suitcases, the hotel offered a final sting in the tail for our Paraguayan experience. Our checking-out time coincided precisely with a power cut. "The lift's not working," I said, pressing the button. "The light's not even coming on. We'll have to carry the suitcases down the emergency exit stairs."

Lugging luggage down a series of never ending narrow steps, especially with people coming up in the opposite direction, was not fun, and by the time we got down, I was panting like a fool. "Bloody Paraguay!" I hissed as I struggled through the small door into the lobby. "We won't be back."

"There are nicer parts of the country though," Angela said as we drove to the airport. "The jungles, for instance: Paraguay has jaguars. I just think Asuncion is horrible. And we were right in the centre of the ugliness." She pointed outside. "Look, this part of the city looks okay."

She was right. Unusually for a capital city, the outskirts were in much better shape than the centre. A plush Sheraton Hotel, a set of car dealerships with brand new cars on their forecourts, and even a modern-looking shopping mall were now on display. Asuncion looked clean and modern, not ugly and battered. Still, I doubted it would be enough to entice tourists.

We arrived at the airport, were stamped out, and waited in the lounge for our flight to Buenos Aires. It was time to tango.

Top row: Presidential palace; Paraguayan militia
Middle row: The view from our hotel; Me, standing in one of
the nicer parts of the city
Bottom row: Monument in the centre of Asuncion; symbol of
Paraguay; Shiny skyscraper

Chapter 7. Tango in Buenos Aires

Interesting fact: In 1892, Argentina became the first country to use fingerprints to identify criminals.

"It's like London or Madrid," I said as we took an evening stroll along one of the main streets of downtown Buenos Aires. The Argentinian capital was in the throes of a rush hour. Yellow and black taxis and modern blue buses plied the busy streets, and the buildings looked large and well looked after. People were rushing by, heading home from work, or else stopping in Starbucks. Buenos Aires was a world away from Asuncion.

Even so, I was slightly disappointed. As we passed upmarket wine shops and busy steak houses, I couldn't shake off the notion we were in Europe somewhere. Even Asuncion had seemed noticeably South American.

"If I took a photo of this street," I said, "and showed it to people back in England. I don't think many would know it was in Argentina."

2

On our first full morning in Buenos Aires, we decided to book ourselves on an organised city tour. With the places of interest in the city spread so far and wide, we thought it would be the best way of seeing the lay of the land, even though we usually scoffed at the notion of sitting in a bus. Alas, though, the big red open-topped bus we'd expected turned out to be a small white minivan full of people who had already hogged the best seats.

"Bloody hell," I whispered, as we took our seats. "This is going to be rubbish. I can tell you that already. We won't be able to see a thing."

Angela shot me a look. "Will you stop moaning, for Heaven's sake? There's not much we can do now, is there? We might as well try to enjoy ourselves."

I sat back as the minivan lurched forward into the traffic. Since leaving the tropics behind in Asuncion, the temperature had fallen drastically. Many people outside were wearing thick jumpers and coats. Even a dog on a lead had a layer of tartan covering its small furry exterior.

"Hi," said the female guide at the front. She had already addressed the passengers in Spanish, and was now relaying the same information in English, presumably just for us. "We will be making three stops on this tour, but as we drive to them, we will pass many more famous sights of Buenos Aires. You will be able to take many special pictures. Before we set off, let's find out where everyone is from."

I rolled my eyes at Angela. It was the tour group bonding session. By the end of the day, we'd all be hugging and exchanging phone numbers.

There were five couples aboard the minibus, including us. One young pair were from Spain, another were from Cordoba, the second-largest city in Argentina. The remaining two couples were from Chile and Colombia. The Colombians were thirty-somethings sitting opposite us.

"Okay, now we all know where we come from, we can set off. Make sure you're all buckled up."

The first thing we saw was the famous obelisk in the middle of Plaza de la Republica. "This plaza," said the guide as Angela and I tried to see past the minibus's bulkhead that blocked all view, "stands in the middle of the widest street in the world. It has nine lanes going in each direction! And the obelisk is amazing, isn't? Please take a photo as we drive past it slowly."

The obelisk was 67 metres tall, but all we could see was the bottom three metres. I tried to move position, but my seatbelt snapped me back into the seat. Angela knew I'd be mad, and she was right. Before I had a chance to remove my shackle and shift for a better position, we were off, heading along one of the eighteen lanes to see the Presidential Palace.

The pink Presidential Palace stood at one end of a large square called Plaza de Mayo. Originally, its hue had come from a mixture of lime and ox blood, but nowadays, the powers in charge of such things used conventional paint.

"We will stop here for twenty minutes," said the woman in charge. "And then we will meet outside that cafeteria, okay?" Everyone looked. The cafe was busy with people buying large ice-creams despite the cool weather. I quite fancied one myself. "Please don't be late because we have a lot to see this morning." Everyone nodded, climbed outside and split up.

"I'm getting an ice-cream," I announced.

"Can't you wait until we've had a look around first?" said Angela, staring up at something called the Piramide de Mayo. It was big and white, with a proud woman at the top; it was the oldest monument in the city.

I unzipped my coat. The sun was coming out and it was getting quite warm. "I suppose so."

Standing outside the palace were a few guards, all of whom seemed happy with people taking photos of them. We walked over to the fence to take some ourselves and then wandered back to the pyramid thing. Just along from it, a large Argentinian flag was flapping in the breeze.

"What are you doing?" asked Angela.

I paused, mid breath, and then continued with my deep inhalation of air. With Angela staring at me, I breathed out. And then I did it again. Afterwards, I said, "I'm checking the good air."

"Good air?"

"That's what Buenos Aires means: Good air. And it is."

"Oh? I didn't know that. But I suppose it makes sense."

I looked at my watch; fifteen minutes had passed already. It was time to make our way to the rendezvous point.

I remembered about my ice-cream. I was about to enter the cafe to buy one when Angela tugged my arm. "It's too late now," she said. "Look, there's the guide."

I turned around and saw her. She was already climbing aboard the bus, and so we followed her and sat down. After a quick head count, the guide spotted the empty seats. It was the Colombian couple. After asking if anyone had seen them, and receiving a set of headshakes in return, she stood at the front and waited. A minute later, she checked her watch and then scanned the street. And then she spotted them, emerging from the cafe scoffing large ice creams.

A professional dog walker, famous in Buenos Aires, was walking by the side of the bus with about twelve large dogs on separate leads. The man seemed in total control of the pack, stopping at a road junction with his horde of hounds obeying his every command. If I'd been in charge of them, I'd be on my stomach being pulled through bushes at top speed.

Our next stop was a football stadium made famous because it was where Diego Maradona used to play. Boca Junior stadium was a large blue and yellow affair with a set of Hollywood-style stars on the pavement outside. We wandered along them until we found the great man himself.

"You can go inside the stadium," said the guide. "But if you do, please be quick. We are only at this stop for thirty minutes."

I looked at Angela, trying to gauge whether she wanted to visit the home of Boca Juniors. I wasn't particularly bothered, but if she wanted to go in, I was happy to do so. She scrunched her face and shook her head, so instead, we browsed some shops opposite. They were full of typical tourist tat, but we bought a few things anyway.

Back outside, we noticed a small crowd had gathered. A man and a woman were dressed up as tango dancers, posing with people for a few pesos. They both looked the part: the man in a dark suit, white collar and black hat; the woman in a black dress and crimson scarf, with her hair tied back tightly in a bun. A man paid for a pose, and while his wife took a photo, the tango lady moved him into position, moving her thigh almost up to his chin. He didn't know where to look.

When our allocated time was up, we boarded the bus again. Five minutes later, the two seats opposite us remained stubbornly empty. After a suitable time of watch glancing, the guide went off to search for them. She returned with the Colombians, who showed not the slightest trace of remorse as they took their seats. As we set off, the man produced a large envelope. Inside was a photo of him and his wife standing inside the stadium holding a huge golden cup. Both stared at the photo and grinned.

5

The guide picked up the microphone. "The next stop is La Boca, the old port area of Buenos Aires. It is where Italian immigrants from the early 1900s settled. The area is famous because of the way the immigrants painted their homes. With leftover paint from the ships, the Italians coloured their houses in reds, yellows, blues and greens. But please do not wander too far from the main street. La Boca is not a safe area for tourists, even during the day. You will be safe on the main street though because there are lots of tourist police."

I'd heard stories of tourists hiring taxis in La Boca, and then being driven just a few blocks away to be robbed at gunpoint. There was no way we would be straying from the main tourist street.

We all left the bus for our final scheduled stop of the tour and took in the surroundings. "Do you know what it reminds me of?" I said to Angela. We were ambling past bars and restaurants painted in gaudy but fetching colours.

"What?"

"A wild west saloon town. All it needs is a sheriff and a couple of horses tied up, and we would be in a cowboy film. I like it."

Plenty of other tourists did too, because the place was packed. And because of the tourists, the touts were out in force. Tango dancing couples were waiting for photo business and cafe touts were handing out flyers. One old man, sporting a grey Father Christmas beard, was the strangest-looking tout of all. He was wearing trainers and black trousers, together with a grandpa-type grey woollen jumper – all very sedate and becoming for the man's age, but it was the red cape and gimp mask that was odd – the mask especially. It covered the top half of his head, with cut out sections for his eyes, and weird antenna-like protrusions sticking out from the top. He was wearing glasses over it, and as we passed, he asked whether we wanted to see a tango show. At least that's what I thought he said.

Other cafes had actual tango dancers cavorting by their entrances to entice people in. Old men with acoustic guitars were sitting near them, playing complex melodies with seemingly little effort or thought. We followed the crowds towards the famous painted houses, noticing that our guide was correct: tourist police were everywhere.

The buildings looked great, almost toy-like. Every brick, stone, wooden beam and corrugated piece of metal had been splashed with bold, bright colours. Together, they looked like an artist's palette. The actual street the buildings were on looked good too, with a series of ornately curved lampposts, sets of wooden benches and scores of art stalls. Paintings of tango dancers, of the colourful buildings, or of Buenos Aires were for sale.

Back at the mini-van, Angela noticed some shoes dangling from the telegraph wires above our heads. There must have been at least a dozen pairs, all of them hanging by their laces. The guide noticed us looking and while we waited for the other passengers to arrive, she explained a little about them.

"I think they might be gang related," she said. "The hanging shoes will separate one gang district from another. But then again, it might just be kids throwing their sneakers up. I'm not sure."

We climbed back aboard the van and sat down. For once, the Colombian couple were there before us. "I know it's a tourist trap," I said, "and I know we could've been robbed just a few streets away, but I think I like La Boca."

"Yeah, me too."

6

That evening, Angela and I visited an upmarket tango house. We paid a premium for it, but it did include a steak meal, all drinks and a couple of hours of tango-tastic entertainment. We took our seats in the main area and sipped on wine while we waited for the main performance to begin. To help pass the time, the tango house management offered some Spanish-flavoured music, as well as a training session for members of the audience, if they so wished.

"Shall we try?" asked Angela.

I looked at the small stage and then at the audience. Some people were talking among themselves, but a large proportion was watching the shenanigans up on the stage. Professional dancers were coaching a few brave members of the crowd, showing them some basic steps and throws. I looked at one man, who looked mightily uncomfortable and shook my head. "Not really. I don't want you to show me up."

Angela took a sip of her Argentinean white wine. "Come on; it'll be fun."

Just then, a tango lady walked up to our table. "You want to try?" she asked.

I shook my head before Angela had a chance to answer. "Maybe later," I said, lying.

"Well, if you change your mind, please ask."

She walked to the next table, but like us, the couple bowed out, as did the next two. She hit the motherlode on the far table though, because all four of them got up. We watched as they tried to follow the complicated instructions, and then laughed as one of the men stepped on an instructor's foot, causing her to shriek.

The meal finished by 10pm and while the plates were being cleared, the tango instructors left the stage. A few minutes later, the lights went down and five white-suited musicians entered from stage right, all men. One sat at a piano, two stood with violins, and a fourth man, the oldest of the bunch, picked up an accordion and sat down. Then he glared at the audience. The final gent was the double bass player who looked like he belonged in a program entitled *America's Most Wanted Serial Killers*. He had long, scraggly hair and sunken eyes, and while he took up station behind his large instrument, he looked like he was dreaming of his grandmother's fingers, the ones that he'd dined upon prior to the performance.

Then after a short count-in, they started playing. They were amazing.

7

The level of musicianship was extraordinary. The five of them swapped between complex time signatures, always a fixture of tango music, and undulating tempos, with total ease and perfection. Even the glare from the accordion player couldn't stop me staring in almost open-mouthed awe at their virtuoso performance.

The dancers came on next, strutting like peacocks. Four women and four men, faces pouting, hips swirling and the clickety-clack of their shoes on the stage mesmerising. Throughout the whole song, they twisted and threw themselves with impeccable timing, exaggerated movements adding drama to the tango.

I could tell Angela was impressed too. Even though the room was less than half-full (it was a Monday night in the winter season), the dancers were still giving it their all. I could see sweat glistening off some of them, and all of them were breathing heavily. I glanced over at the upright bass player and caught him staring at the accordionist's fingers.

At the half way stage, forty minutes in, a newcomer came to the stage. Like a heavy metal guitar god, the longhaired, middle-aged gent strolled to the front of the stage with an eight-stringed miniature guitar. The dancers left the stage and the five musicians stopped playing. After staring at each member of the audience, he threw back his head and let rip.

Like a demented Latino Jimi Hendrix, the man contorted his face and stamped his booted feet, swaying and rocking, all the while playing a tune. Suddenly, without any warning whatsoever, he turned and rushed towards the accordion player, shouting something at him in Spanish. The old man stared back, and, for a moment, I thought he was going to throw his accordion at him. Instead, he looked down and then started playing, his instrument offering a pleasing accompaniment to Mr Long Hair's playing. Soon, the other musicians joined in, building to a conclusion involving many false endings and raucous foot stamping before finally ending to rapturous applause. The man bowed his sweat-drenched head and then left the stage.

I needed a drink of wine after all that, and while I poured Angela and myself a glass, the dancers returned for the second half of the show. It was just as good as the first, with only one schmaltzy moment right at the end. During the encore, as the band had struck up the opening chords to *Don't Cry For Me Argentina*, a couple of crooners entered the stage. And for the next five minutes, they sang a cringe-worthy rendition of the famous hit.

"So that's a tango dance crossed off the list of things to do while in South America," I said as we headed outside to the line of waiting taxis. "And I've got to say: I enjoyed it more than I thought I would."

"I loved it," agreed Angela. "But I knew I would. It was a real highlight of our trip."

8

The next morning, Angela and I were inside a graveyard. This was no ordinary boneyard though, because the Recolata Cemetery was more like a gothic-tinged mini town, all contained within a high wall. Huge mausoleums belonging to the rich and famous of Buenos Aires filled the cemetery.

Almost all of the mausoleums looked like small houses, and were much taller than us. Many were adorned with concrete angels and glass panels, and all of them looked expensive. One mausoleum looked like the cover of a horror film DVD. Cobwebs covered its black wooden doors, and I could easily imagine a horrible thing breaking through the glass in the dead of night.

Angela and I were seeking out one particular mausoleum, that of Eva Peron (otherwise known as Evita), the charismatic wife of ex-president Juan Peron. Peron had been the revered leader of Argentina in the 1940s and 1950s, and his wife was equally as popular, due to her beauty, intelligence and kindness. Evita died of cancer, aged only 33, and when her death was announced to the Argentine population, the country went into shutdown. Millions lined the streets of Buenos Aires, wanting to mourn the president's wife.

Eva Peron's body was embalmed, and a huge monument was planned as her mausoleum. Unfortunately, though, a military coup then took place in Argentina, causing Juan Peron to flee to Spain. In his haste to escape, he had to leave his wife's body behind.

The new government removed Evita's body from its mausoleum. Then, for the next sixteen years, its whereabouts was unknown. All across Argentina, officials tried to stamp out any lingering displays of affection for the old regime, and made it a crime to say the names of the former president and his wife.

In 1971, Evita's body was found in a crypt in Milan. Juan Peron had it flown to his home in Spain, where he kept the embalmed body on display on a platform in his dining room. What his new wife thought of this arrangement was anybody's guess. Two years later, Peron made a triumphant return to Argentina and became president once more. Soon after, Evita's body returned too, eventually ending up in the Recolata Cemetery.

9

"Where is it, then?" I said as I studied the map. Every lane seemed to end up at another lane, which then fed off into even more lanes. The Recolata Cemetery was a labyrinth.

"Give me the map," snapped Angela, finally losing patience with my woeful skills at navigation. I handed it over, spotting two fluffy cats tucked down one of the side avenues. They were both asleep about a metre apart from each other.

"It's down there," said Angela, pointing past the cats.

"It can't be."

"Why not?"

"Because the guide book said there would be crowds of people. And there's no one there."

Angela studied the map again and walked off, sending the cats scurrying for cover. I followed her, shaking my head – we were nowhere near the final resting place of Eva Peron, I was sure of it. After a few seconds, Angela stopped walking and pointed. "There," she said. "Eva Peron."

Damn. She was correct. It was the grave of Eva Peron, part of the Duarte mausoleum (the maiden name of Eva Peron), and unlike all the other grey and white tombs, this one was clad in black marble. Someone had placed a single red rose on the front of the tomb.

"Her mausoleum is supposed to be booby trapped," I said. "It has trapdoors and false coffins."

"Why?"

"Maybe because they were scared of her body going missing again."

We stared a few moments longer and then made our way out of the huge maze of tombs and gravestones.

10

We headed back into the city centre, once more walking along streets that could have easily been in most European capital cities. Downtown Buenos Aires was packed with shoppers and pedestrians because of a tube drivers' strike: in its fourth day, according to a newspaper I'd read. Eventually though we arrived at the Plaza del Congreso, a large open space with an enormous statue of a woman in the middle, and the colossal Congress Palace (for which the square was named) at one end. A set of benches surrounded the statue, and on them were a few homeless people, all of them asleep. The previous night, Angela and I had seen a few people near our hotel, foraging through the city's refuse bins. Every city seemed to have homeless people, but Buenos Aires seemed to have more than most.

Angela insisted we visit a large shopping mall, which, due to the strike, ended up taking about an hour to reach. When we arrived, Angela caught me rolling my eyes at the array of shops and shiny escalators. She knew I was not a fan of shopping. "Why don't you sit in that Starbucks," she suggested, "while I go and look around a few shops?"

"A few?"

"Yeah. I'll only be about half an hour or so. You can get a coffee and go on the internet."

Sighing, I nodded. I entered the cafe, ordered a latte and then sat down. Then I got up to ask the young man behind the counter for the wi-fi code. He shrugged apologetically. "There iz no wi-fi today. Iz out of order."

I nodded and returned to my seat. Par for the course. After drumming my fingers, and then taking a few sips of my coffee, I got up again, this time to grab a free newspaper from the stand. In the course of my travels, I'd often found that amusing stories could be found in local newspapers.

I opened the Buenos Aires Herald and found the main story was focussed on the tube strike, which it described as a 'living hell' for the city's commuters. I flicked through the rest of the newspaper but found nothing of interest. I drummed my fingers some more and then played a stupid game on my phone. I became so absorbed in it that I didn't notice when Angela returned, empty-handed as usual.

"Did you have fun?" I asked.

Angela sat down and briefly looked at the newspaper. "It was okay. I just don't like it when shop assistants follow me around. They do that a lot here."

"Do you know what I'm looking forward to?"

Angela raised her eyebrows.

"Steak. Prime Argentinian steak."

"Oh yeah. Me too. Let's go back to the hotel and get changed. Then we'll get some beef."

11

The steak was divine. The thick cut of prime beef arrived with a generous side helping of French fries and salad. Not the healthiest meal we'd had in South America, but certainly one of the most delicious.

Argentina is the fourth highest beef consumer in the world (after the United States, Brazil and China), and its history is steeped in cattle production. Ever since the Spanish introduced cows to Argentina in the sixteenth century, gauchos have bred them, cooked them and put their tasty steaks onto plates.

"Mmmm," cooed Angela. "This is one of the best steaks I've ever had. It's even better than that one we had in Asuncion."

I nodded, unable to answer. My mouth was full of succulent beef, cooked to perfection by the restaurant's chefs. After I'd swallowed it, I smacked my lips together in satisfaction.

Buenos Aires had ended on a high after a fairly lacklustre start.

Top row: Plaza de Mayo; A local beer and a delicious steak!
Middle row: The Mausoleum of Eva Peron; dog walker of Buenos Aires; Impressive statue in Plaza de Congreso
Bottom row: One half of the world's widest street (note the giant obelisk and an image of Eva Peron); Painted houses of La Boca;

Chapter 8. Watching Montevideo

Interesting fact: Uruguay's official name is the Oriental Republic of Uruguay.

The flight from Buenos Aires to Montevideo took less than one hour and we landed straight into a rain-drenched Uruguay. Thankfully, by the time we had been processed through the modern airport, we could see slithers of blue poking through the grey. It was the start of what would turn out to be a very pleasant day in the Uruguayan capital. I turned to Angela and handed her my passport for safekeeping. "I think we're going to like Montevideo."

Sitting in the back of an airport taxi, heading towards the centre of the city, I recalled watching a memorable episode of The Simpsons. Homer finds a globe and, after turning it, notices Uruguay. Guffawing, he says, 'Look at the name of this country! U R Gay!' It was an amusing moment, and I never thought for a moment I would be in that actual country.

Montevideo (translating as: look at the mountains) was a strange name, I thought, because Montevideo didn't even have any mountains; it only had a small hill overlooking the bay. But the name originated from the 16th century when Portuguese explorers, who had been sailing down the River Plate, had noticed the hill. One man yelled that he could see a mountain and the name stuck.

The road we were driving along seemed modern and well maintained. The buildings by the side were large and modern, though some did feature thatched roofs. We could also see the hill that the explorers had once mistaken for a mountain. They must have been delirious, because it was definitely a hill. We forked right along a pleasant coastal road offering an expansive sea view on our left-hand side. Montevideo reminded me of a British seaside town and I pointed out the similarity to Angela. The only things spoiling the illusion were the palm trees and flocks of small, green parakeets.

2

Montevideo's old town was where most of the tourist attractions were, but before going there, Angela and I decided to get some lunch in a shopping mall opposite the hotel. As we ascended the escalators, I was delighted to find a clothes shop very much to my liking. Its name was very short but very effective: *TITS*. I couldn't resist the urge and whipped out my camera to take a photo. As I did, with Angela laughing behind me, a woman walked past and glanced at me, then in the direction of my lens. She shook her head and carried on. Undeterred, I framed my shot and it was a good one. Tits to be proud of. I wondered whether to go in to feel the merchandise.

Despite being in one of the steak capitals of the world, after eating so much of the stuff over the past few days, we decided to go to a pasta bar. Uruguay's teenagers made it almost impossible to find a seat, but we managed to find a plastic bench in the end.

"In two days time, we'll be sitting on Cococabana Beach," I stated.

"Copacabana Beach."

"Yeah, Cococabana Beach."

Angela shook her head. "Are you doing it on purpose?"

I was nonplussed. "Doing what on purpose?"

"Saying it wrong."

"Saying what wrong?"

Angela put her fork down and looked at me. "Which beach are we staying at?"

"I've told you. Cococabana."

"No! It's Copacabana! C-O-P-A-cabana," she said, spelling out the first four letters. "Not C-O-C-O-cabana. I thought you were saying it wrong back in Bolivia, near that Lake Titicaca town."

I scowled. "So that song by Barry Manilow is wrong? *At the Coco, Cococabana, the hottest spot north of Havana."*

"No, Barry Manilow didn't get it wrong. His song was called *Copacabana*. It's you who is wrong, and I can't believe you don't know how to say it properly. It reminds me of that time you were looking for a new watch last year, and you noticed that all the watches in the shop were showing a quarter to five. You asked me whether the hands had been set to that particular time on purpose, remember? You thought they maybe showed the hands in a *good light."*

I nodded and took a mouthful of pasta.

"But then you realised the time was actually a quarter to five. Idiot. So say the beach again," my wife asked.

"Copa-cabana."

"Correct. Hallelujah!"

"Okay, you can shut up now. You're starting to annoy me."

3

Foolishly, we assumed the walk to the old town would take us about ten minutes because on the map it looked like it was just around the corner. But an hour later, after passing a statue of a poet and spying numerous palm trees, we were still only about halfway there.

The views were great though, offering golden beaches, a fair smattering of skyscrapers and some cormorants and herons out in the surf. Power joggers and cyclists were out in high numbers too, sometimes making stops at the free exercise equipment the town planners had provided. "I can't believe nobody is on the beach," said Angela, removing a stone from one of her sandals.

"It's because it's winter. Just wait until the summer; the place will be packed. Apparently, these beaches are popular with people from Buenos Aires."

We came to a strange monument dedicated to victims of the WW2 Holocaust, a strange thing to have in South America, we both thought. We stopped and stared at a section of broken railway track and then at some stone slabs, all of them overlooking the grey expanse of ocean. Later, we found out that Uruguay had once possessed a thriving Jewish population, mainly from the 1920s and 1930s, when people arrived from Russia and Germany. Often they were just passing through on their way to Argentina, but enough of them stayed to produce a sizeable community in Montevideo. One of them was a fifteen-year-old girl called Ana Balog. For some reason, she returned to Hungary in 1945 with her father but was captured by the Nazis. They both died in Auschwitz.

Twenty years later, Montevideo was the scene of a daring Nazi killing. Mossad agents lured a Latvian Nazi called Herberts Cukurs to the city. During the war, Cukurs' nickname had been the Butcher of Riga because he had overseen the deaths of thousands of Latvian Jews. When the war ended, Cukurs escaped to Brazil where he secured himself a job as a pilot, his pre-war profession. He did quite well by all accounts, until someone persuaded him to travel to Montevideo to secure a business deal. When he arrived at a house in a city suburb, someone shot him in the head at close range. Israeli agents claimed the death as theirs, saying justice had finally been served.

4

"We should've caught a taxi," Angela said, stopping to shake even more stones from her sandals.

"There's no point now; we're nearly there." We had stopped near a wall overlooking the water. On the other side of us were the buildings of downtown Montevideo. To get a taxi now would be a waste of money.

Five minutes later, we saw a signpost pointing to Independence Square, the heart of the old town. With weary limbs and aching feet, we turned away from the coast and headed inland.

The first things we saw in the square were a massive Uruguayan flag flapping in the light breeze and a massive statue of a man on a horse. But then our eyes were drawn to the building at the far end of the square. It was the Salvo Palace, a grey building with a bulbous tower. It used to be the tallest building in South America. In the overcast conditions, it looked unsightly and perhaps even ghoulish, but it definitely stood out. Underneath it, businessmen and businesswomen passed with a blur of briefcases and dark suits, as did a troop of uniformed schoolchildren under the direction of a harried-looking teacher.

"Who is he?" asked Angela, gazing up at the statue.

"Jose Gervasio Artigas," I said. "The national hero of Uruguay."

"How do you know?"

I pointed at the pedestal. "It says there."

"Why is he the national hero?"

I shrugged. "I'm not sure. Let's get a coffee and I'll find out."

5

Artigas was born in Montevideo in 1764. When he was a young boy, his parents sent him to a religious school for his education but at some point, Artigas swapped his Bible for a set of strong ropes and became a cattle rustler. It wasn't long before a bounty was on his head. With a life of crime ahead of him, and with the authorities permanently on his tail, it seemed that Artigas's life was heading for disaster. Except it wasn't. Great things were about to happen to him, all thanks to the Anglo-Spanish War.

With British warships patrolling the sea around Montevideo, the local Spanish viceroy offered Artigas (now in his thirties) a deal. He told Artigas that the bounty would disappear if he agreed to help fight off the Brits. Artigas accepted the deal and discovered he possessed great military skill. The British were defeated, and Artigas rose through the ranks of the army to become one of the most famous military tacticians in Uruguayan history. The remains of the great man lie under his statue in a mausoleum.

"Wow," said Angela. "From cattle thief to army general: a real rags to riches story."

"Yeah, but it didn't really end well for him, though. He ended up in exile in Paraguay where he died."

"Poor man. Ending up in Paraguay."

"His remains only came back to Montevideo in 1977."

6

Away from the central square, Montevideo was like any other large city. Department stores, fast food joints (including McDonalds and Burger King), people handing out flyers and teenagers chatting into mobile phones all added to the hustle and bustle. Taxis were hawking for business and buses were chugging their way along the streets. Some stalls were selling roasted almonds and we stopped to buy some. Angela tasted them, deemed them delicious and so we carried on eating them as we walked.

"Have you noticed," I said between mouthfuls, "that everyone looks European here?"

Angela stared about at the people: the shoppers, peddlers, cab drivers, people carrying brief cases, and even the heavily-armed police officers who seemed to be everywhere. Long gone were the indigenous people we had seen so often in Bolivia and Peru. In fact, as in Buenos Aires, we could've been in Europe.

7

The next morning, we awoke to rain. Instead of hunkering down in our room though, Angela and I donned caps, capes and brollies (so to speak) and left the hotel – destination: a mall Angela had noticed on the map

As we traipsed along in the gloom, cars and buses tried to splash us while hidden cracks in the pavements attempted to lure us into watery traps. Somehow we avoided getting drenched, and passed embassies, expensive houses and then, further along, a huge white cross with a statue of Pope John Paul II underneath. Water dripped from his outstretched hand and papal mitre.

The mall wasn't as good as the one we had visited the previous day. Angela quickly deemed it worthy of only a cursory browse, which was fine by me; after a quick coffee we studied the map again, and decided to walk to the Legislative Palace, mainly because the map designers had provided an illustration of it. From its little picture, it looked grand and stately.

We traipsed along a rough-looking street full of broken pavements and graffitied walls. Thankfully, the rain had ceased, but there was still a dull light cast upon the city to make the place feel unwelcoming. We had turned off the main road, taking a shortcut to the palace. Stray cats lounged about in alleyways and dog mess was everywhere. But even worse was the litter – it was as if someone had emptied a bin, allowing the contents to fly free. Rusty cars parked by the side of the road added to the unwelcome feel. "It reminds me of Asuncion."

I negotiated a large puddle. A piece of flotsam lingered on the surface. It looked like a Snickers wrapper. A rusted horse-drawn cart trundled past with a couple of men sitting at the front. Behind them were bags of garbage.

Walking more quickly, we left the grim street behind and arrived into an open space where, thankfully, the litter and rundown buildings were no more. The only building of note was the one we'd been looking for: the Legislative Palace.

Striking columns and stately windows faced us from the enormous white construction, the place where the Uruguayan parliament met. Whether it was in session, we couldn't tell, but we did notice the solitary guard watching us.

"Why is he just staring?" asked Angela. "Are you sure we're allowed to take photos?"

I lowered my camera and looked over at the man. He had a large weapon and a fixed expression. "Photo okay? I shouted towards him. "Si, photo?"

The man shook his head, grabbed his automatic weapon and fired twice. One salvo landed by my feet, the other shattered the camera lens. Except they didn't. The guard merely nodded. We thanked him and took a few more, and then wondered where to go next.

8

Five minutes later, we found ourselves near an abandoned train station. If the earlier street had reminded us of Asuncion, then this new area cemented the impression. Why the station was derelict, we had no idea, but we could see that it did provide an area of slumber for the homeless. Groups of unfortunates sat huddled under plastic sheets or rough-looking blankets. Some shouted at us as we rushed past, but we didn't linger long enough for any of them to get up.

"Where are we going?" asked Angela. We had crossed over a railway line and seemed to be in some sort of dockland area. Long lines of parked trucks were waiting to unload and receive cargo. Montevideo was one of South America's major ports, the main reason the city had been founded.

I looked at the map. The road running parallel to the port should lead us back into old town. I told Angela this. She looked around, first at the neglected railway tracks, then at the massive abandoned station. A metal fence surrounded it. She looked at me. "You always manage to find the nicest parts of a city, Jason, you really do."

We set off walking, finding ourselves eerily alone. All the waiting trucks were empty, and no one seemed to be in any of the cargo areas. The port area was a ghost town. Suddenly, from a fenced-off gate, two men appeared. Both were in their early thirties, wearing thick coats against the winter of Uruguay. They walked towards us, hands deep in their pockets.

Angela edged closer to my side as the men approached. Both were staring at us and I wondered what was in their pockets. We quickened our pace slightly, not saying anything, the distance between us shortening with every step. I put my own hands in my pocket, clasping my wallet tightly. The men were less than five metres away.

"Hola," one said cheerfully, smiling at us.

"Hola," I replied, as they passed. A couple of seconds later, I turned and saw them climb into one of the trucks. Instead of being marauding bandits, the duo had simply been delivery men.

9

Back in the central square, the sun came out. It was amazing what a bit of yellow light could do to liven up a place. In the gloom, the Salvo Palace had looked like a concrete monstrosity, a tower of Victorian nightmares, but now, with a healthy glow upon it, it was a majestic building that drew the eye rather than offended it.

"What are they drinking?" I asked Angela. A passing man was carrying a cup of green stuff. He wasn't the only one. He had a metal straw stuck into his mouth and seemed to be sucking up pond water for enjoyment.

Angela shook her head. "It looks horrible."

Nearby, a group of workmen were idling during their lunch hour. All of them had mugs of the stuff, and one man had a thermos flask, which he was pouring into his and his pals' mugs. The mugs looked like they were made of wood, covered with intricate patterns. Montevideo seemed in the grip of green soup fever.

10

Along the busy pedestrian-only street, we found what we were looking for – a stall selling wooden mugs and metal straws. Ahead of us, a teenage girl had stopped at the stand and was actually buying some of the green stuff. Transaction complete, she wandered away, heartily sucking from a straw.

The green liquid turned out to be mate (pronounced matt-ay) a type of herbal tea with a strong caffeine kick. To enjoy it (we later found out) a person would place healthy amounts of dry mate leaves into the bottom of a wooden mug. Then, after adding hot water (usually from a flask), the brew was good to go. I asked the man behind the counter about the possibility of tasting some.

The man shook his head. "Is no possible to try. Only to buy." He pointed at the small bags filled with green leaves. The girl we'd seen earlier must have simply bought a bag of mate leaves to put in her pot.

I looked at the bags. I didn't really want to buy a collection of green leaves just for the sake of it. What would I do with them? We thanked the man and walked away.

A few minutes later, we found another mate stall. It had the same array of wooden mugs, metal straws and packets of leaves. But unlike the first man, this vendor actually had a mug of mate in his hand. As he watched our approach, he took a swill of it.

"Hi," I said, smiling. "Do you speak English?"

"Si," he said, putting the mug down.

"Great! My wife and I are leaving Montevideo tomorrow, but before we go, I'd love to try some mate."

The man regarded us. For a moment, I wondered whether he was going to tell us to get lost. "Of course," he smiled. "Try some of mine, senor. Here."

The man passed me his carved wooden pot. The metal straw was dunked into what looked like a pile of wet leaves. The mug felt warm and the smell from the mate reminded me of green tea.

I glanced at Angela and then I sucked up a tentative amount of the liquid, expecting to find grit and leaf pieces entering my mouth. But the mate came out lump free and tasted of what I'd thought it might – green tea, but with a bitter, almost coffee-like taste. It wasn't bad, but it certainly wasn't anything I'd be in a major rush to try again.

"Good yeah?" asked the grinning man.

I nodded. "Very nice."

I handed the pot back to the man who placed it on his counter. "Is very good for you. Helps clean liver and kidney. And do you know something? In my country, a person is on their way to have mate, are having mate, or have just left some place where they've just had mate."

I thanked the man for his generosity. We headed back to the central square.

11

"Well that's Montevideo done," I said. We were walking towards a parked taxi. "And I've quite enjoyed it."

We got in the taxi, giving the name of our hotel to the driver. He nodded and set off just as a cloudburst sent a wave of drizzle over the streets of downtown Montevideo.

"You Americano?" asked the driver, a man in his forties.

"No. We're from England," Angela told him.

"Ah, England! Long way to come! Tell me, why you in Montevideo?"

"On holiday. We came from Buenos Aires."

The driver considered this, turning along a road running parallel to a large golf course. "Montevideo is much different from Buenos Aires, yes? Much smaller."

"Yeah," I said. "Which in some ways is better."

"So you like Montevideo?"

"Yeah. The coastal road is really nice and the old town is good. So yeah, we're glad we came."

Ten minutes later, the taxi pulled up outside our hotel. Despite knowing we were foreigners and staying at a nice hotel, the driver charged us the correct tariff. We thanked him and rushed into the foyer.

Before arriving in Montevideo, we'd heard that the city's inhabitants could be a little unfriendly and distant, but judging from the people we'd met on our short visit, this notion was wrong. Everyone we'd come across had smiled and said hello. Even the vagabonds had waved. In fact, it was one of the friendliest countries we'd been to.

Once more, we packed our bags, checked our passports, confirmed flight times and organised a taxi to take us to the airport the next day. It was almost time for the final leg of our South American journey – Rio de Janeiro.

Top row: Salvo Palace; Looking out over Montevideo
Middle row: An interestingly named clothes shop; Street scene
from downtown Montevideo
Bottom row: Impressive Legislative Palace; Jose Gervasio
Artigas monument; Along the coastal promenade

Chapter 9. Coca, Copacabana!

Interesting fact: About a fifth of Rio de Janeiro's population lives in favelas (unregulated housing often called slums).

Our hotel was located on Copacabana Beach, and from our balcony we could see not only the long strip of yellow sand edging the gorgeous expanse of blue ocean, but also, high on a hill, the white statue of Christ the Redeemer, something we would be visiting a few days later.

"This is amazing," beamed Angela as we stared out over possibly the most famous beach in the world, and one I had only recently learned to say correctly. Red parasols covered every inch of the sand (apart from where volleyball matches were taking place), and bronzed beach bodies filled in the gaps. "How lucky are we?"

"I can't believe this is our final stop before going home." Half of me was glad that we were going back to England, back to normality, but the other half of me, the traveller part, wanted to carry on to places such as Venezuela, Colombia and Chile. But all trips must eventually come to an end, and where better to finish ours than in Rio de Janeiro.

After breakfast, we headed straight for the beach. It was everything we had imagined Rio to be – the sand, the Atlantic and the long line of plush hotels, all with a backdrop of lush tropical hills and peaks. The only thing that shocked us was the number of whales.

We had expected beach babes and muscle hunks on Copacabana Beach, but about half of the people lounging around were flabby-bellied and lard-arsed.

"Look at her," I said, pointing to a woman about to enter the ocean. She was huge, with rolls of flesh wobbling with every step. Despite this, she had somehow squeezed herself into the smallest green string bikini possible. And she wasn't the only one. But at least they all had a tan.

We carried on along the beach, kicking sand beneath our feet and avoiding the men selling beach towels, sarongs and umbrellas. Then we began to notice a few honed bodies among the blubber. A set of young women wearing black sunglasses were stretched out in the sun looking like Formula One models, and further along, another two gorgeous young ladies were laughing as they sipped on coconut milk. A trio of young men jogged past us, all muscles and shades, white teeth and designer stubble. Another couple of toned men were doing pull ups on some strategically-placed bars. Everywhere was the sound of laughter, of waves or of light aircraft as they pulled banners across the sky.

2

Angela and I walked onwards to Fort Copacabana, a military museum. It stood on a headland at the end of the beach. The Brazilian government had built the fort at the beginning of the 20th century to protect the city's harbour from invaders, but in 1987, they decommissioned it and turned it into a museum.

The path leading up to the museum was littered with cannons and various other pieces of small artillery. A guard stood to attention near the entrance, and after paying the small fee, we were in, wandering around a series of rooms displaying what life had been like inside the old fort. As both Angela and I were self-confessed museum heathens, we quickly tired of the displays, and so ventured outside so we could climb the battlements. As well as a few sturdy bastions, and some massive guns that seemed to be pointing towards Sugar Loaf Mountain, there wasn't much there.

The view was great, though. We could see the whole stretch of Copacabana Beach and the glorious mountains beyond. And then Angela spotted something. It looked like a squirrel but it wasn't. It was a marmoset.

The tiny monkey looked like a cross between a squirrel and a gremlin, and it preferred hiding rather than posing for a photograph. The one we'd noticed ran like the clappers until it reached a small stone bridge, where it adroitly scurried underneath, hiding itself in the beams. While we waited, camera poised, it occasionally poked its small head out to look at us, its inquisitive eyes regarding our faces for a second. Then it was gone.

"Right," I said. "I'm going to zoom in and wait for it to appear. Even if it only shows up for a nanosecond, I should get it." Angela nodded, straining forward too.

For five minutes I stood as still as I could, camera zoomed in, arms held steady. It didn't look out once. I held my stance, even with my arms shaking from trying to hold the camera still for so long. Perhaps the marmoset had gone, I thought. I lowered the camera.

"There it is!" said Angela. I raised the camera but it was too late; it had hidden itself back in the beams. I zoomed in again and waited. And waited some more. When my arms started trembling for a second time, I lowered the camera. That's when it reappeared.

"Little swine," I screeched when it did it for the third time. It was as if it knew.

Angela decided to step over some safety ropes to get closer to it, but an eagle-eyed security guard spotted her immediately. He blew his whistle and made a dramatic arm motion for her to cross back over. Angela did so, cursing the guard while I cursed the marmoset.

We admitted defeat and walked away. As in Panama City with the sloth, we were almost at the exit to the fort complex when Angela spotted another one, this one agilely running along a telegraph wire, great shocks of white frizz sticking out from the sides of its head. It stopped at the halfway point and looked down at us. This time I was prepared and snapped a quick photo. It was slightly blurred, so I thought I'd try another, this time zooming in. While my lens whirred and whizzed, the marmoset stayed satisfying still, and then, as I pressed the button, it scarpered. It looked like it was mocking me.

3

On the other side of Fort Copacabana was another of Rio's famous hotspots – Ipanema Beach (the world's sexiest beach, according to the Travel Channel). It was even busier than Copacabana, full to the brim with bronze. As we wandered along the sand, men hollered for our attention, wanting us to sit on one of their sun loungers, or trying to tempt us into buying a pair of sunglasses. Half-way along, we stopped at a stall to buy a coconut. The man in charge nodded, picked up a green coconut, lopped off the top, stuck a couple of straws in and then handed it to us. The liquid inside was delicious and pleasingly cool.

"Rio is in my top ten," said Angela as she took another sip. Overhead, the sightseeing helicopters and banner-towing light aircraft were still buzzing the skies. "I can see why the rich and famous come here. It's gorgeous."

A couple of police officers wearing shorts and shades passed us. The police had a high presence in Rio, we had noticed, making sure the beaches and tourist areas were clear of potential felons. Crime, unfortunately, was a part of life in Rio de Janeiro. Behind our hotel, away from the coast, we'd already seen banks with fortress-style security doors and armed guards. We had also come across a few people who had looked at us in a way that suggested they were appraising our worth. But for now, we walked along Ipanema Beach, revelling in the fact that we were walking on one of the most famous stretches of sand on the planet.

4

The next day, after a morning spent sunbathing on Copacabana Beach, Angela and I waited in the hotel's lobby. Although not fond of organised tours, especially after our experience in Buenos Aires, both of us felt that the easiest way to see Christ the Redeemer, the massive white statue standing on Corcovado Hill, was by signing up for one. Besides, the brochure described the tour as, '*a quick drive from your hotel to the Cosme Velho Train Station. From there, you will ascend by cog train through the Tijuca Forest, the largest urban rainforest in the world. From 2300ft height above sea level, you will be at the steps of Christ, where you will have breathtaking views of Rio de Janeiro below*'.

If I had written the blurb, mine would read:
'*After picking up a coach load of pissed-off passengers (who have been driven around ten hotels already), you will begin your journey through the less interesting parts of Rio de Janeiro. Don't bother to take a photo! After thirty minutes, we will deposit you outside an untidy train station where you will queue for half an hour in the heat, before joining a stampede for the train. Once you have taken your seats (if you are one of the lucky ones!), you will ascend through some pleasant scenery, pausing to stop at obscure places for no apparent reason. Twenty-five minutes later, you will arrive at the top, where you will have precisely thirty minutes to take in the views before joining the horrendous queue to get back down. At the bottom, you will board your coach and wait for forty furious minutes until the passengers (who failed to catch the correct cog train!) arrive with you. Then you will be driven back to your hotel. Thirty minutes of pleasure for three and a half hours of pain. Book now! Special discount!*'

5

The views were spectacular though: a panorama of Rio and the Atlantic beyond, all under the gaze of the gigantic white statue of Jesus Christ. It really was the only redeeming feature of the trip. The viewing platform was jam-packed, crawling with people, some even lying on their backs to get the best photo angle of the statue. But who could blame them? Christ the Redeemer was truly iconic, a white giant of a man, the second largest statue of Jesus anywhere in the world (the biggest one is in Poland). It even had a small chapel inside its base.

Even more people were pressed together at another viewing platform, this one looking down upon the city. Jostling, pushing and shoving were going on in a paparazzi-like scrum. Smiling people, pretending they were having a good time as others people tried to barge them sideways, posed at the edge. Angela and I found a quieter spot and gazed down. Rio de Janeiro looked amazing, a hodgepodge of white skyscrapers, golden beaches, blue ocean and tropical highlands. With our thirty minutes almost up, we joined the queue for the cog train down the hill.

6

The next morning, we discovered that as well as its beaches, Rio also possessed a fine set of colonial buildings, including theatres, fountains, libraries and banks. They were all located well away from the beaches in a downtown part of the city. It was a side of the city we hadn't expected. The Opera House had apparently been modelled on one in Paris.

Angela and I were on another organised tour, this time on our way to visit Sugarloaf Mountain. Not long after setting off from the hotel, we had passed one of Rio's famous favelas, noticeable because of the tall concrete walls surrounding the hillside shanty dwellings.

"Some of you may have noticed the favela up there," said the guide, another bilingual woman with a microphone. "They began showing up in Rio's suburbs in the 1970s, though their origin dates from a century earlier."

The woman told us that typically (though not always) favelas are under the control of major drug traffickers. For this reason, the crime rate is high. These drug lords will have vast power over large areas of the shanty dwellings, often living luxurious lifestyles within them. With their private armies, they will offer 'security' to their neighbouring citizens. If a resident chooses not to pay for this protection, then their property is fair game. Unsurprisingly, most people pay the drug lords, especially since they also provide bus transport, power and even children's entertainment. Yet despite this outward show of community spirit, these criminal bosses would think nothing of killing anyone who stood in their way. The favela kings rule the shady underworld of Rio de Janeiro slums with a rod of iron.

"Slum tourism is very popular," said the guide. "Organised tours take people inside a place called Rocinha, the largest favela in Rio. Tourists can see for themselves what it is like to live there. Some of you may be wondering what the drug gangs think of this? Oddly enough, they like the tours because they show the favelas in a favourable light: citizens enjoying samba classes, children playing on bouncy castles, the tour shows that Rio's favelas are not all rampaging neighbourhoods of gunfights and mass drug taking. In fact, some of the money that these tours generate goes towards building orphanages and schools."

We passed the favela on the hill and carried on towards the centre of the city.

7

Rio de Janeiro's financial district was full of modern skyscrapers, but we bypassed the glass and glamour to stop at one of the ugliest churches we had ever seen.

"We will stay here for twenty minutes," said the guide, in Spanish, English and German. "If you are late back to the coach, we will not wait for you. We have a tight time schedule for the cable car ride up to Sugarloaf Mountain."

Everyone climbed off the coach and gathered outside Rio Cathedral, a great whack of grey concrete that had been blackened and dirtied since its construction in the 1970s. It had supposedly been built in the style of a Mayan pyramid, but that seemed unlikely to me; it was more like an overgrown multi-storey car park, and not a very nice one at that.

As ugly as the exterior was, the interior was beautiful. The pyramidal shape and the mass of stained-glass windows made it almost breathtaking. So the designers had known what they were doing after all. Angela and I wandered around, occasionally taking photos of the windows, until we arrived back at the entrance.

Back aboard the coach, we were surprised when everybody arrived back on time. Five minutes later, we were driving towards the cable car station.

8

The journey up the wires was fun, offering the expected superb views, but the vista from the top was even better. Across from us was Christ the Redeemer, the tiny white figure with his hands spread wide easily recognisable. Below us were the beaches and skyscrapers, as well as one of the city's airports. It looked like a toy town version of a landing strip. A constant stream of airliners was descending past Christ, circling over the bay, and then coming in to land.

Conveniently, the people in charge of the viewing area had provided an overpriced cafe. After buying ourselves an ice-cream, we sat down, admiring the view. "What is a sugar loaf?" Angela asked.

Surprisingly, I knew the answer. "In the 16th century, when the Portuguese were in charge, traders used to leave pots of sugar by the harbour to be loaded onto ships. The pots were cone shaped and called sugarloaves. They looked quite similar to the shape of this mountain. So that's why they named it."

We finished our ice-creams and wandered back to the viewing platform. Another airliner was making its approach across the bay below us, and a few minutes later, it landed with a puff of wheel

smoke. Angela turned to me. "Rio is not in my top ten any more –
it's in my top five. Just look at it."

I stared out. It was one of the best views we had seen. I nodded.
Rio was incredible.

9

The afternoon was spent back on Copacabana Beach. It was our
last few hours in Brazil, and once more, the beach was full of
bronze bodies, either sunbathing, flying kites, or power jogging.
Angela and I found a quiet spot, lowered the sun loungers, donned
some shades and enjoyed the sun. It was hard to believe it was the
middle of winter!

An hour later, while Angela went off for a dip, I got chatting to
a middle-aged American man sitting on the next sun lounger. His
name was James and he was from Chicago. He was travelling
alone and had been to Santiago, Buenos Aires and now Rio.

"I made a stop at Iguazu Falls," he told me. "The falls straddle
three different countries: Brazil, Argentina and Paraguay. Have
you been to Paraguay?"

I nodded and told him of our short time in Asuncion. He
snorted. "You managed a day, huh? I managed one hour."

James told me that while in Iguazu, he'd seen tour guides
advertising day trips to Paraguay. Not wanting to pay the big bucks
being asked for, he decided to hire a taxi and go there himself.

"This cab driver said it would be thirty dollars, there and back,
which I thought was reasonable. Twenty minutes later, we arrived
at the border and the first thing I saw was a cop with a huge gun.
That set the scene for what was to come. The Paraguayan border
town was a mess, with broken-down buildings and a ton of garbage
on the floor. People were hanging around, nothing to do, just
staring at me. I had a quick walk around and then got back in the
cab. 'Take me back,' I told the driver. 'I'm not staying in this God-

forsaken place.' He laughed and did just that. A few days later, I flew to Rio. I love it here."

And that was the thing about Rio, both of us agreed: anybody who visited the city could not help but fall in love with it. It was one of those cities that seemed to have everything. No wonder it had been picked to host the 2016 Summer Olympics.

A couple of hours later, back in the hotel, Angela and I began packing our suitcases for the last time on our trip. After twenty-three days, our South American adventure was almost over. But what a trip: seven countries, ten cities, two Wonders of the Modern World and no lost suitcases. The highlights had definitely been Rio de Janeiro, Cusco, Machu Picchu and Peru as a whole. We'd also loved Lake Titicaca and the scenery of Bolivia, but had been less enamoured with La Paz. We had been pleasantly surprised by both Panama and Montevideo, but Asuncion we could forget all about. As for Buenos Aires, we had enjoyed it, but had failed to see the beauty that most others had seen. We packed our things, collected our passports, and headed to the airport for the flight back to Europe.

"I don't think we've become jaded," said Angela as we sat in the departure lounge. "I've loved it in Rio. Waking up in a hotel overlooking Copacabana Beach was the best thing for me. Seeing Sugar Loaf Mountain...it was all amazing. Even Asuncion was an experience – not one I want to repeat – but still an experience. I think travelling to so many different places makes us appreciate the great places even more. I think, if anything, we are guilty of forgetting how bloody lucky we are."

I nodded. Angela was right. South America had been fantastic and we were not world-weary travellers. I sat back in my seat and smiled, wondering which part of the world would be next on the list. That made me excited.

Top row: The majesty of Rio de Janeiro; Christ the Redeemer; The beaches of Rio
Middle Row: Rio Cathedral; The bronze bodies of Brazil
Bottom Row: Copacabana Beach; Angela at the top of Sugarloaf Mountain

Read the first chapter of Flashpacking through Africa by Jason Smart. Available at Amazon in paperback or on Kindle.

.

Flashpacking through Africa

Travels through 17 African Nations

By Jason Smart

Published by Smart Travel Publishing

Chapter 1: Charmless Charmers and Unsavoury Guides

Interesting fact: The Shrine of Sidi Yahya, in Eastern Morocco, reportedly contains the tomb of John the Baptist.

"Hello!" said the man in the long blue robe and charcoal headcovering. His black beard and dark features added stark contrast to his royal blue neck scarf. He looked about thirty years of age.

Angela and I were walking towards Marrakech's old town. We'd just visited Majorelle Gardens, owned by none other than Yves Saint Laurent, and we wanted to get to the central square for a coffee, before hitting the souqs.

"I am not guide," the man said in broken English as he walked alongside us. "I only wish to practise English with nice people. Perhaps I talk with you?"

For most of the day, Angela and I had been hassled by people left, right and centre. They were trying to either sell us something, or guide us somewhere we didn't want to go. *'I take you to tanneries!'* was a common opening gambit, referring to the place where animal hides were prepared in Marrakech. Another was, *'You want hashish? I get you good hashish!'* But this was always directed at me. The snake charmers in Djemaa el Fna, the central square, had already ripped us off too. After draping snakes upon our heads and shoulders, then taking a few photos (with our camera), the charmless charmers had demanded money.

"Four hundred dirham!" one of the men had said with a toothless grin. All around us was a cacophony of musical instruments and banging of drums, as well as the clickety-clack of carts being pushed towards the souqs. A man with two monkeys waited nearby, trying to entice another couple into posing with them.

I looked at the snake charmer and shook my head. Four hundred dirham was about thirty pounds. "No way."

Both men looked offended. "Yes! We take many photo!" one of them said. "Four hundred dirham is price. You pay right now!"

After a few minutes of haggling, we relented and gave them two hundred. We would have given even less had we possessed smaller notes. If only we'd visited one of the orange juice stalls that lined the square to get some change first. Lesson one learnt: carry small value notes in Morocco. And with the man in blue trailing after us, we were about to learn lesson number two...

2

"My name is Muhammad, and I am Berber," he said. "You must be heading for square. I take you there as gift."

Berbers were the indigenous people of North Africa. They had lived on the edge of the Sahara for centuries. Historically, Berber tribes had been farmers and nomads, but in modern times, many had moved into the cities. Muhammad was one of them.

Angela and I said nothing. Doing so would only bring about more talk of tanneries or perhaps of a cousin's lamp shop. We carried on walking, hoping he'd take the hint. Ahead of us, a large woman in a headscarf mounted a motorbike and then, with a blast of power, she was off.

Unofficial guides were a problem in Marrakech. In fact, they had become such a major irritant to tourists that the authorities had been forced to act. Undercover police patrolled the old town as well as key places of interest, searching out unofficial guides and removing them if found. But in other parts of town, like the one we were now in, men such as Muhammad had a free rein.

Crossing a road, we quickened our pace. Muhammad stopped on the other side shaking his head. "If heading to square..." he shouted. "You go wrong way! Square this way! Please come! I show you!"

We ignored him. We hurried along a street full of metalwork and hardware shops. Some of the copper kettles outside one shop were enormous.

"Okay," said Muhammad after catching up with us. "We get to square this way. Take longer that is all."

3

Ahead of us were the salmon-pink walls of the old city, stretching for nineteen kilometres. Made of red clay and chalk, Marrakech's old town was called the *Red City,* and it wasn't hard to see why. Angela and I headed towards a busy gate cutting through the 30-foot walls, hoping it would lead us to the central square. Muhammad doggedly stuck to our side.

The gate was crowded with hawkers trying to sell sunglasses and cheap watches, but we passed them and entered the medina within. Narrow, stone alleyways with cobblestone floors cut their way through stone arches and clay buildings. A horse and cart stood just inside the entrance; its cargo of chickens creating a hullabaloo until we passed it. It was like stepping back in time.

"Many buildings were homes of rich men," Muhammad said jovially. "Wealthy men would own a few buildings, all close together. One would be for him and his wives, the others for his concubines." Muhammad looked at me, grinning. "Good life, eh!"

I had to admit that Muhammad seemed a knowledgeable fellow, and he certainly seemed friendly enough. Plus, it was interesting having him around to point things out that we would have ordinarily missed. How much was true, however, was anyone's guess.

"Come," he said. "I show you university. Is very beautiful building. You take many good photo. Then I take you to square."

I looked at Angela and shrugged. We followed our new guide through the rabbit warren of the northern medina, a labyrinth, every turn taking us deeper within. A few small stores sold grocery products, and above our heads, clothes dangled from wooden awnings. Suddenly a donkey clattered past, heavily laden with goods for the market, its owner sitting on the edge of his cart.

"This is old university," said Muhammad when we arrived at a small square. The three of us stopped to admire the buildings around the edge. Arches that looked like oversized keyholes and beautifully patterned walls made the small square a delightful sight. "It used to hold nine hundred students but was closed in 1960," explained Muhammad. "It is now a historical building."

After taking some photos we all moved off, with Muhammad now firmly in the lead.

4

The crowds thinned out. We followed the man in blue, wondering when we would get to the central square. We were in his hands now, and that was that. In a quiet alleyway, Muhammad sidled up to me. "You are not first people I help in Marrakech. And even though I not *official* guide, people often pay me for my time and kindness." He smiled. "Perhaps you will pay me later - if you wish - but before that, let me tell you something of my people, the Berber."

Muhammad informed us that the Berber people were fine artisans but had a big problem in Marrakech. "The authorities will only allow four days in whole year when we can sell the goods we make. So you are lucky to be in Marrakech today! It is Berber selling day! Come, I show you!"

We didn't feel lucky. Muhammad probably wanted to show us his brother's fabric shop or his uncle's leather store. We came to a more populated part of the medina where people sat about in doorways drinking tea and smoking cigarettes. Some individuals even waved at Muhammad. Others simply stared at Angela. We didn't have a clue where we were.

After a short while, Muhammad stopped outside a dingy-looking shop. It looked like someone's house, except for a few carpets dangling outside the door.

"This is quality Berber carpet shop," said Muhammad. "I not make money for bringing you here - that I promise - I just want you to see fine quality of artisan. Come, come, follow please!"

I could tell that Angela had had enough of the charade. And I felt the same. We had no interest in carpets, Berber or otherwise.

"No," I said, standing our ground. "We just want to get to the square."

Muhammad smiled disarmingly. "Yes, but carpets are of finest quality. You do not have to buy. Just look. Please come! Only for one minute"

I shook my head. "No."

Muhammad paused for a moment, seemingly at a loss, but then quickly regained his composure. "As you wish. You do not like the carpet, I understand. I take you to square. Please come." We left the doorway and followed him down yet another alleyway.

5

Muhammad seemed less jovial than before. Perhaps he realised we were not going to visit any of his *"brother's"* stores. In a deserted alleyway, he stopped and turned to face us. "I am good guide, yes?"

We stopped, and Angela nodded uncertainly.

He said, "Yes, and people pay me for being good guide. They always very generous. You pay me now!"

I shook my head. "You haven't taken us to the square, so why should we pay you?"

"Because I take time to show you old town."

I took Angela's hand, and we walked past him. We quickened our pace, hoping to come to a more populated part of the medina, perhaps even one we recognised. Muhammad caught up with us. This time he raised his voice. "You pay now!"

We ignored him until we arrived at another crossroad of alleyways. There were a few people in sight, and so we stopped to face our tormentor. For all I knew, he had a knife hidden in his robes somewhere.

"How much do you want?" I asked

"Four hundred dirham."

Four hundred dirham again, I realised. It seemed the standard rate for ripping off tourists in Marrakech.

"No way." I said, fishing about in my pocket for some small change. "You can have twenty and be done with it."

"*Twenty!* I cannot feed my family for that. You must give four hundred."

I shook my head and handed him a twenty note. "That's all you'll get. Take it or leave it."

Surprisingly, Muhammad accepted the note and pocketed it within a second. "Okay, square that way. Good-bye." And with that, he disappeared from sight.

Lesson number two had been a good one: trust no one in Marrakech.

6

In times gone by, the heads of executed people were placed on spikes in Marrakech's main square. This grisly fact was the reason Djemaa El-Fna had gained its name: *gathering place of the dead*. Nowadays though, the square was a hive of activity, apparently the busiest in all Africa. Angela and I were sitting in a rooftop cafe overlooking it all.

Stalls ranged from the relatively normal (shoe shiners, women selling henna patterns, spices and oils) to the rather bizarre (tiny tortoises or plastic world leaders relentlessly driving jeeps and tanks around circular tracks). And then there were the freakish items (false teeth and goat skulls). The sounds were equally exotic. They sounded like the Marrakech of my imagination - an orchestra of bizarre musical instruments with some percussion provided by the hooting of motorcycle horns. It was the perfect soundtrack to what we could see below.

Easily visible from the square, and indeed most of Marrakech, was the Koutoubia Mosque, the tallest building in the city. In fact, local statute dictated that no other building could ever be higher than the mosque, making Marrakech a distinctly low-rise city.

"I'm not sure whether I like this," I said to Angela as I poured myself another glass of mint tea. I placed the silver teapot back on its tray and took another sip. Even though I found the taste quite refreshing, the amount of sugar in the drink was too much for me.

Angela nodded absent-mindedly. I could tell she was still thinking about Muhammad, and how he'd led us on a merry old dance around the medina. "People like him just spoil it," she said. "Pressuring us into giving them money. It's not fair."

I stared down at a donkey pulling a cart filled with tin pots. Motorcycles and taxis were driving through one end of the square, the road not even marked. How people were not injured or killed was a mystery, but somehow it worked. There was a certain order to the chaos.

"I know," I said, putting my glass down next to the teapot. "But we knew this would happen. And now we know what to say if we meet another one - which we will. We've just got to be firm and tell them to get lost."

Angela nodded and took a sip of her Diet Coke.

7

To cheer ourselves up, we decided it was time to hit the famous souqs, the main tourist attraction of the city. In the centre of the square, spilling out into the medina in all directions were bewildering arrays of stalls, from tiny cupboard-sized kiosks selling nuts and spices, up to gaudily stocked fabric shops that seemed to increase in size once over the threshold.

The crowds pushed us along, and every now and again a hoot from behind would make everyone move to the side as a motorbike snaked its way past. A clanging bell indicated a donkey and cart were coming through. Bags, belts, shoes, carpets, and wooden handicrafts were everywhere to see. The smell of spices hung in the air and outside every shop sat a man waiting to pounce.

"Hello," one man boomed. He sat outside a stall peddling shoes. "I have good bargains here. I give best price! Look inside…come!"

Our eyes met for half a second and he jumped up, beckoning us towards his store. "Come in! See my quality footwear!"

We ignored him and walked on.

At a leather bag store, we decided to stop. Angela quickly spotted something she liked. The proprietor grinned a happy grin when she asked to feel it.

"This is quality leather product," he said, getting it down with his hook. "Very high quality, made only from finest leather."

Angela felt the leather and turned the bag over in her hand. "Yes, it's nice."

The man flashed dollar symbols in his eyes. "Yes, very nice!" He was grinning like a Cheshire cat.

"How much?" Angela asked.

The man shrugged and looked coy. "Madam, you give me fair price!"

Angela looked at me. I regarded the bag and decided to offer him a pathetically low amount just to see what he would do. "One hundred dirham," I said, about eight pounds.

The man's look of utter shock confirmed that the game was on, as did the uproarious laughter that followed. "One hundred dirham would not even buy a piece of rough leather! This bag is worth over six hundred dirham! But…because today has been slow day, I will sell it to you for five hundred. That is best price!"

Angela didn't say anything and so he looked at me to see what I thought about his offer. To me, £40 for a bag seemed a bit steep so I shook my head.

The man furrowed his brow and raised his palms upwards. "But five hundred dirham is best price! The leather is best quality. Please feel it, sir!"

"No thanks," I said, playing my part in this well-rehearsed haggling dance. "Come on," I said to Angela. "Let's try somewhere else."

Angela nodded and handed the bag to the man, but of course he refused to accept it. "Okay, four hundred dirham," he said. "That is final price."

Angela looked at me. I could tell she thought it was a fair price.

"No, it's too much," I said. I took the bag from Angela's hand and placed it on a nearby table. As we turned tail the man spoke again. "Okay please stop! Offer fair price! Remember, I am a humble shop keeper with children to feed!"

"One hundred and fifty dirham," I stated, looking the man in the eye.

"Three hundred and fifty!" he countered.

I shook my head. "Two hundred."

"Please, sir!" the man wailed, picking up the bag again. "The leather alone is worth more than two hundred dirham! I will lose money! The bag is yours for three hundred dirham!"

I shook my head and led Angela out of the shop. The man followed us out. "Okay, wait! Two hundred and eighty dirham."

"Two hundred," I stated again.

"Please, sir! I cannot sell the bag for such a low price. My children will starve! Meet me half way, and pay two hundred and forty."

"Two hundred and ten."

"Two hundred and thirty."

We shook hands on two hundred and twenty dirham. A fine dance it had been.

8

That night, Djemaa el Fna Square was even busier. The snake charmers had mostly departed, as had the monkey handlers, and now it was the turn of the street entertainers. Various crowds had gathered around them, and we strolled over to one group to watch two Berber musicians playing traditional instruments. One was a flute-like instrument, the other like a small banjo. The sound they created was distinctly Moroccan and pleasantly exotic.

Some crowds assembled around acrobats and storytellers; others favoured the spectacle of magicians or medicine men. Angela and I left the musicians and stopped to watch the strangest display of all. It was a man dressed as a woman cavorting and spinning like a transvestite from hell. He'd squeezed his large frame into a golden dress (adorned with dangling but highly percussive accessories) and was dancing about to a rhythm created by a second man playing a tambourine. He floated around the circle to much applause and laughter, rippling his belly for comic effect. A third man hovered at the periphery, eyeing new people to approach with his tray. After depositing a few coins, we were off towards the centre of the square, the home of the outdoor eateries.

Smoke billowed upwards from the brightly-lit food stalls, creating a translucent mist that cloaked the minaret of the Koutoubia Mosque. We chose a stall near the edge of the vast eatery section, mainly because of its spare seats. Quickly a tray of olives came, then some flat bread and a bowl of spiced sauce. A cat joined us underfoot just as the meat kebabs arrived. The meat was cooked to perfection and tasty as hell.

"Sorry, cat," I said as I took another mouthful of skewered kebab. But then guilt got the better of me. I bit off a small section and dropped it down. The tiny piece of meat disappeared and a second later, the cat resumed its imploring upwards look.

"I see the appeal of Marrakech now," said Angela, also dropping some meat down for the cat. "This square is amazing.

The food, the performers, the souq, and best of all, no unofficial guides. This is why people should come here."

9

Our riad was just minutes away from the square. The word *riad* literally translated as: *house with an interior garden*. When we'd first arrived in Marrakech, the taxi driver had stopped at the end of a narrow alleyway, telling us to follow him on foot because it was too thin for his vehicle to fit down. Unused to this sort of service from a taxi driver, but thinking it wise to heed his instruction, we followed the man until we reached a large wooden door. Entering, we couldn't believe that such a beautiful place could exist within such dimly lit alleyways. We paid the driver and he nodded and bowed, pocketing his money.

Our ground floor room was on the edge of a small courtyard. A trickling fountain lay in the centre. Our heavy wooden room door would keep out intruders, but the windows would offer no such protection because instead of glass, they utilised heavy fabric curtains. Luckily they only overlooked the central section of the riad, and not the alleyway outside.

"Well today was okay actually," said Angela, poring over the booty we'd bought in the souq earlier. Bags, shoes, belts, ornaments, and a red fez that I already regretted buying littered the room.

"Yeah, it was," I said, picking up a lamp and turning it around so I could study the work that had gone into it. The proprietor had said that four individual artisans had been responsible for it, and I had no reason to doubt him. My only concern was fitting everything into our luggage.

"And I'm glad we started in Morocco and not somewhere else," said Angela. "I think Marrakech has given us a good idea of what's to come in Africa. Come on, let's get some sleep."

10

The next morning we ventured up to the rooftop breakfast area. Chattering birds and busy streets indicated that Marrakech had woken well before us. After finishing our breakfast of fried bread and delicious dips, we walked over to the rooftop edge. Between the satellite dishes and telephone wires, Marrakech looked ancient. It was time to head down into it.

Along a back alleyway close to the medina, we found two cats. One was a mangy-looking ginger animal chewing on a discarded chicken head, but next to it was perhaps the most pitiful cat we'd ever seen. Matted fur covered a rake-thin body, its tail blackened from all the puddles it had trailed through. But its eyes were the worst thing. One was permanently closed while the other looked like it had been gouged out. The thing's ears twitched as I bent to give it some bread. It gobbled it down in a second. I wondered how it survived.

"Hello," said a man's voice.

We turned to see a young man wearing jeans and a T-shirt. He was smiling.

"Do you need any help today? Perhaps to see the tanneries, or maybe to visit where carpets are made?"

Angela stiffened and shook her head. I shook mine too. "No, we don't need a guide, thank you. And don't bother following us please. We are fine by ourselves. Do you understand?"

The man raised his hands in acquiescence. "Of course."

We walked away, and the man didn't follow.

11

Undiscovered until 1917, the Saadian Tombs were now a major tourist attraction of Marrakech. They contained over a hundred and fifty graves of rich Moroccans.

Inside, visitors were wandering the gardens to admire the plaster archways, or else gazing at the centrepiece, the Chamber of the Twelve Pillars, the final resting place of Sultan Ahmed el-Mansour, the man who commissioned the tombs. The shaded mausoleum featured highly-decorative tiles, both on the floor and walls, as well as the twelve marble columns that had given it its name. Before French archaeologists had rediscovered the tombs, the area had been a slum area.

"Who was the sultan?" asked Angela.

We found a shaded spot where I got the guidebook out. Overhead a small lark flew past, before landing on a nearby wall. The Saadian Tombs were proving to be a peaceful oasis amid the commotion outside.

"It says he was an early 17th century Sultan who died of the plague. But before that, he was good at organising battles. He spent most of his money on these tombs and on a palace."

Not far from the tombs was a rooftop terrace with a nice little cafe. As we sipped our drinks, we could see large storks sitting in gigantic nests on the top reaches of some buildings. Storks were revered in Marrakech, we knew, and harming one carried a stiff, three-month prison sentence. Just then, one flapped its long wings and took off, heading in the direction of the square.

Our time in Marrakech was almost at an end, and I asked Angela what she thought the highlights were.

"The souqs," she answered straightaway. "All that haggling and all those leather bags! I loved it. The food was good too."

I took a sip of my cola. "My favourite thing was the central square. I could've stayed there all day, just watching what was going on."

Angela nodded. "Those donkeys around the edge were so cute."

We finished our drinks and made our way back to the riad to pack. It was almost time to visit the second African nation of our tour: The Gambia.

If you have enjoyed reading Panama to Rio de Janeiro, then perhaps you will enjoy the author's other travel books. All are available on Amazon.

The Red Quest
Flashpacking through Africa
The Balkan Odyssey
Temples, Tuk-Tuks and Fried Fish Lips
Panama City to Rio de Janeiro

Visit www.theredquest.com for more details.

Printed in Great Britain
by Amazon